The Best Test Preparation

CAHSEE

Mathematics

Stephen Hearne, Ph.D.
Professor of Psychology
Skyline College
San Bruno, California

Edited by Penny Luczak, M.A.

Research & Education Association
Visit our website at
www.rea.com

Research & Education Association
61 Ethel Road West
Piscataway, New Jersey 08854
E-mail: info@rea.com

THE BEST TEST PREPARATION FOR THE CAHSEE EXAMINATION IN MATHEMATICS

Printed in the United States of America

Library of Congress Control Number 2004095859

International Standard Book Number 0-7386-0000-8

REA® is a registered trademark of
Research & Education Association, Inc.

ABOUT OUR AUTHOR

Stephen Hearne is a Professor of Psychology at Skyline College in San Bruno, California, where he teaches Quantitative Reasoning, Experimental Psychology, and General Psychology. He earned his B.A. from the University of California at Berkeley in 1982, his M.A. from San Diego State University in 1987, and an M.S. in Marriage, Family and Child Counseling from San Jose State University in 1992. He earned his Ph.D. degree from the University of Mississippi in 1998, specializing in Quantitative Psychology. For the past twenty years, Stephen has tutored students of all ages in math, algebra, statistics, and test preparation. He prides himself in being able to make the complex simple.

ABOUT OUR EDITOR

Penny Luczak received her B.A. in Mathematics from Rutgers University and her M.A. in Mathematics from Villanova University. She is currently a full-time faculty member at Camden County College in New Jersey. She previously worked as an adjunct instructor at Camden County College as well as Burlington County College and Rutgers University.

ABOUT RESEARCH & EDUCATION ASSOCIATION

Founded in 1959, Research & Education Association is dedicated to publishing the finest and most effective educational materials—including software, study guides, and test preps—for students in middle school, high school, college, graduate school, and beyond. Today, REA's wide-ranging catalog is a leading resource for teachers, students, and professionals. We invite you to visit us at _www.REA.com_ to find out how "REA is making the world smarter."

ACKNOWLEDGMENTS

In addition to our author and editor, we would like to thank Larry B. Kling, Manager, Editorial Services, for his editorial direction; Diane Goldschmidt, Project Manager, and Gianfranco Origliato, Project Manager, for their editorial contributions; and Jeff LoBalbo, Senior Graphic Designer, for providing pre-press electronic mapping. Supervising press readiness was Pam Weston, Production Manager.

CONTENTS

PART 1: Number Sense   1

PART 2: Measurement and Geometry   13

PART 3: Statistics, Data Analysis and Probability   31

PART 4: Algebra and Functions   41

PART 5: Algebra I   59

PRACTICE TEST 1   77

PRACTICE TEST 2   139

A Note from the Author

This test preparation and review book will help students successfully pass the California High School Exit Exam in Math. It was specifically written for the current test using the CAHSEE Mathematics Blueprint, which was finalized by the California State Board of Education in October 2003. The blueprint is a public document, published by the California Department of Education, Standards and Assessment Division.

For the most part, this book is structured in the form of questions and their solutions. However, some units simply provide examples of important mathematical formulas, operations, and problem solving strategies. This book also includes two complete practice tests designed to strengthen learning and to assess the student's current level of math proficiency.

A test preparation in the truest sense, this volume is not a substitute for a math textbook or the wisdom of a classroom teacher. This book teaches all of the mechanics required with the ultimate goal of passing the CAHSEE exam.

Prerequisite: This book assumes that the student knows his or her multiplication tables.

Stephen Hearne, Ph.D.

Independent Study Schedule

Week 1	*Study Part 1. Be sure to thoroughly work through all the tasks and questions given. If you have particular trouble with any of them, go back and study the corresponding section of the review.*
Week 2	*Study Part 2, and be sure to complete all tasks and questions. If any particular type of question gives you trouble, review that section again.*
Week 3	*Study Part 3, and be sure to complete all tasks and questions. If any particular type of question gives you trouble, review that section again. Have a teacher check your work.*
Week 4	*Study Part 4, and be sure to thoroughly work through all the tasks and questions. If you have any problems, work through the drills more closely.*
Week 5	*Take Practice Test 1, and after scoring your exam, review carefully the explanations to the questions you missed. If there are any types of questions that are particularly difficult for you, review those subjects by studying again the appropriate section.*
Week 6	*Take Practice Test 2, and after scoring your exam, review carefully the explanations to the questions you missed. If there are any types of questions that are particularly difficult for you, review those subjects by studying again the appropriate section.*

CAHSEE

Passing the
CAHSEE Mathematics
Exam

Passing the CAHSEE-Math

About this Book

This book provides you with an accurate and complete representation of the Mathematics section of the California High School Exit Examination (CAHSEE). Inside you will find reviews that are designed to provide you with the information and strategies needed to do well on the test. Two practice tests are provided, both of which are based on the official CAHSEE. The practice tests contain every type of question that you may expect to appear on the CAHSEE Math. Following each test, you will find an answer key with detailed explanations designed to help you completely understand the test material.

About the Test

Who Takes the Test and What is it Used For?

Beginning with the class of 2006, every high school student who plans to graduate from a California public high school must first pass the California High School Exit Examination (CAHSEE). The test consists of two parts: Mathematics and English-Language Arts.

Students are first required to take the CAHSEE in grade 10. If you pass both the Mathematics and the English-Language Arts section, you will not be required to retake the test. If you pass only one section, you must retake the other part in grades 11 and 12, until you pass. If you do not pass either part of the CAHSEE, you get the chance to retake both sections in grades 11 and 12, until you pass.

When and Where Is the Test Given?

Every public school district in California has to provide students with multiple opportunities to take the CAHSEE. Your high school may choose from a list of test dates for administering the CAHSEE that are designated by the State Superintendent of Public Instruction. Your school is also responsible for accommodating the test-takers. The questions and scoring guides are provided by Educational Testing Service.

The CAHSEE test is administered over two days. The English-Language Arts section is given on the first day followed by the Mathematics portion the next day.

The CAHSEE is an untimed test, so if you need until the end of the school day to finish, take the time.

Is There a Registration Fee?

No. Because all California public high school students are required to take and pass this test in order to receive a high school diploma, no fee is required.

Special Test Arrangements

Parents of special education students, students with disabilities, and students who are learning English should contact their local high school officials regarding possible waivers or special arrangements, such as the use of a calculator when they take the CAHSEE. In order to be considered for a waiver, students must be diagnosed with a physical or learning disability or be in the process of learning the English language.

Additional Information and Support

Additional resources to help you prepare to take the CAHSEE include the official State of California CAHSEE website at http://www.cde.ca.gov/ta/tg/hs and REA's *The Best Test Preparation for the CAHSEE English-Language Arts*.

How to Use this Book

What Do I Study First?

Read over the reviews and the suggestions for test-taking. Studying the reviews thoroughly will reinforce the basic skills you need to do well on the test. Be sure to take the practice tests to become familiar with the format and procedures involved with taking the actual CAHSEE.

To best utilize your study time, follow our CAHSEE Independent Study Schedule located in the front of this book.

When Should I Start Studying?

It is never too early to start studying for the CAHSEE. The earlier you begin, the more time you will have to sharpen your skills. Do not procrastinate! Cramming is *not* an effective way to study, since it does not allow you the time needed to learn the test material. The sooner you learn the format of the exam, the more time you will have to familiarize yourself with the exam content.

Format of the CAHSEE Math

The Mathematics portion of the CAHSEE is designed to test the following skills:

- *Statistics, Data Analysis, and Probability:* These questions deal with statistical measurements, data samples of a population, theoretical and experimental probabilities, and data sets with one or more variables.

- *Number Sense:* These questions deal with properties of rational numbers and fractions, exponents, powers, and roots.

- *Algebra and Functions:* These questions deal with quantitative relationships, integer powers, simple roots, graphing linear and nonlinear functions, and simple equations and inequalities.

- *Measurement and Geometry:* These questions deal with units of measure, ratio conversion, changes of scales, the Pythagorean theorem, and computing perimeter, area, and volume.

- *Mathematical Reasoning:* These questions deal with approaching problems, determining that a solution is complete, and using strategies, skills, and concepts.

- *Algebra I:* This section deals with finding the reciprocal, taking a root, the rules of exponents, absolute values, expressions and inequalities in one variable, multi-step problems involving linear equations and inequalities in one variable, graphing linear equations and computing the x-and y-intercepts, verifying that a point lies on a line, the relationship of parallel slopes, systems of two linear equations, solving a system of two linear inequalities in two variables, performing basic operations on monomials and polynomials, and applying algebraic techniques to solve rate, work, and percent mixture problems.

There are a total of 80 multiple-choice questions with four answer choices on the math section of the CAHSEE. They break up as follows:

Skill Tested	Number of Questions
Statistics, Data Analysis, and Probability	12
Number Sense	14
Algebra and Functions	17
Measurement and Geometry	17
Mathematical Reasoning	8
Algebra I	12

Scoring the CAHSEE

In order to represent a consistent level of achievement for each administration of the test, and because the questions may differ on each version of the CAHSEE, a constant scale was developed by the makers of the test. The scale ranges from 250 to 450 for each test. You will need a score of 350 to pass the math part of the CAHSEE. Though the raw score corresponding to the 350 mark may vary from one test to another, the scaled score of 350 will always measure the same level of difficulty. Since this statistical scale cannot be duplicated in this book, the chart included in this book represents the scoring of the practice tests only, not the actual exam.

Total Scaled Score

The raw score for each practice test is determined solely by the number of questions answered correctly. Using the chart included in this book, convert your raw score into a scaled score. Accordingly, in order to achieve a passing score of 350, you must answer 44 questions correctly.

Scoring your practice tests

For each practice test, you will have two scores: the raw score, which will be determined by the number of questions answered properly, and the scaled score, which can found using the table in this book. The score you earn on our practice tests should approximate the score you will receive on the CAHSEE.

About the Review Sections

The review in this book is designed to help you sharpen the basic skills needed to pass the Mathematics Section of the

CAHSEE. You will find test-taking strategies, a review of arithmetic, algebra, geometry, and word problems, and questions and tasks to strengthen your abilities in these areas. By using the reviews in conjunction with the practice tests, you will better prepare yourself for the CAHSEE itself.

Test-Taking Strategies

Although you may not be familiar with standardized tests such as the CAHSEE, there are many ways to acquaint yourself with this type of examination and help alleviate your test-taking anxieties. Listed below are ways to help you become accustomed to the CAHSEE, some of which may be applied to other standardized tests.

What to Do Before the Test

- **Pay attention in class**.

- **Carefully work through the review sections of this book.** Mark any topics that you find difficult, so that you can focus on them while studying and get extra help if necessary.

- **Take the practice tests and become familiar with the format of the CAHSEE.** When you are practicing, simulate the conditions under which you will be taking the actual test. Stay calm and pace yourself. After simulating the test only a couple of times, you will feel more confident, and this will boost your chances of doing well.

- **Students who have difficulty concentrating or taking tests in general may have severe test anxiety.** Tell your parents, a teacher, a counselor, the school nurse, or a school psychologist well in advance of the test. They may be able to help you learn some useful strategies that will help you feel more relaxed, so that you can do your best on the test.

What to Do During the Test

- **Read all of the possible answers.** Just because you think you have found the correct response, do not automatically assume that it is the best answer. Read through each answer choice to be sure that you are not making a mistake by jumping to conclusions.

- **Use the process of elimination.** Go through each answer to a question and eliminate as many of the answer choices as possible. By eliminating two answer choices, you have given yourself a better chance of getting the item correct since there will only be two choices left from which to make your guess. Sometimes a question will have one or two answer choices that are a little odd. These answers will be obviously wrong for one of several reasons: they may be impossible given the conditions of the problem, they may violate mathematical rules or principles, or they may be illogical.

- **Work on the easier questions first.** If you find yourself working too long on one question, make a mark next to it on your test booklet and continue. After you have answered all of the questions that you know, go back to the ones you have skipped.

- **Be sure that the answer oval you are marking corresponds to the number of the question in the test booklet.** Since the multiple-choice sections are graded by machine, marking one wrong answer can throw off your answer key and your score. Be extremely careful.

- **Work from answer choices.** You can use a multiple-choice format to your advantage by working backwards from the answer choices to solve a problem. This strategy can be helpful if you can just plug the answers into a given formula or equation. You may be able to make an educated guess based on eliminating choices that you know do not fit into the problem.

- **If you can not determine what the correct answer is, guess anyway.** The CAHSEE does not subtract points for wrong answers, so be sure to fill in an answer for every question. It works to your advantage because you could guess correctly and increase your score.

The Day of the Test

On the day of the test, you should wake up early (it is hoped after a decent night's rest) and have a good breakfast. Make sure to dress comfortably, so that you are not distracted by being too hot or too cold while taking the test. Make sure to give yourself enough time to arrive at your school early. This will allow you to collect your thoughts and relax before the test, and will also spare you the anguish that comes with being late.

CAHSEE Raw Score to Scaled Score Conversion

Scale Score	Raw Score	Scale Score	Raw Score
250	0	344	41
250	1	346	42
250	2	348	43
250	3	350	44
250	4	352	45
250	5	354	46
250	6	356	47
254	7	358	48
260	8	360	49
264	9	362	50
269	10	364	51
273	11	367	52
277	12	369	53
280	13	371	54
283	14	373	55
287	15	375	56
289	16	378	57
292	17	380	58
295	18	382	59
298	19	385	60
300	20	388	61
303	21	390	62
305	22	393	63
307	23	396	64
310	24	399	65
312	25	402	66
314	26	406	67
316	27	409	68
318	28	413	69
320	29	417	70
322	30	422	71
324	31	427	72
327	32	432	73
329	33	438	74
330	34	445	75
332	35	450	76
334	36	450	77
337	37	450	78
338	38	450	79
340	39	450	80
342	40		

*Due to the statistical formulas used by Educational Testing Service, your performance on our practice tests can only *approximate* your performance on the actual CAHSEE Math; one will not directly equate with the other.

CAHSEE

Part 1:

Number Sense

NUMBER SENSE

UNIT 1

1. THE LOWEST COMMON DENOMINATOR

Task: Add two fractions together.

$$\frac{1}{3}+\frac{1}{4}=$$

Solution: When adding or subtracting fractions you need to find the lowest common denominator. The **lowest common denominator** is the smallest number that can be divided by both denominators. First, find the lowest common denominator between the two fractions. In this case, the common denominator is 12 because both 3 and 4 divide evenly into 12. In order to change the two fractions into fractions that have a common denominator, multiply the top and bottom of the first fraction by 4. Then, multiply the top and bottom of the second fraction by 3. Lastly, add the two fractions together.

$$\frac{1}{3}+\frac{1}{4}= \qquad \frac{4\times1}{4\times3}+\frac{3\times1}{3\times4}= \qquad \frac{4}{12}+\frac{3}{12}=\frac{7}{12}$$

2. COMPUTATIONS

All of these are different notations for representing 2 times 3. They all equal 6.

$$2\times3 \quad 2*3 \quad 2(3) \quad 2[3]$$

Other computations: When multiplying fractions, multiply the top times the top, and the bottom times the bottom. When dividing fractions, multiply the first fraction times the second fraction turned upside down, called the reciprocal.

$$\frac{2}{3}\times\frac{4}{5}=\frac{8}{15}$$

$$\frac{3}{8}\div\frac{2}{7}= \quad \frac{3}{8}\times\frac{7}{2}=\frac{21}{16} \quad \text{or} \quad 1\frac{5}{16}$$

3. CONVERTING A FRACTION INTO A DECIMAL AND A PERCENT

Question: What is $\frac{3}{4}$ in decimal form?

Answer: Divide the top number by the bottom number.

$$\frac{3}{4} = 4\overline{)\begin{array}{l} .75 \\ 3.00 \\ \underline{2.8} \\ 20 \\ \underline{20} \\ 0 \end{array}}$$

Task: Convert the decimal answer that you just got into a percent.

Solution: Move the decimal point two places to the right.

$$0.75 = 75\%$$

Note: 1% of something represents one-hundredth of something or 1/100. 10% of something represents one-tenth or 1/10. 25% is one-quarter or 1/4. 50% is one-half or 1/2. 75% is three-quarters or 3/4. And 100% of something is 1.0 or all of it.

Question: What is 75% of 80?

Answer: The word "of" means multiply.

$$\begin{array}{r} 80 \\ \times\,.75 \\ \hline 400 \\ 5600 \\ \hline 60.00 \end{array}$$

4.   FINDING THE PRIME FACTORED FORM OF A NUMBER

Finding the prime factored form of a number means breaking it up into parts. A **prime number** is a number that can only be divided by 1 and itself. The following are examples of prime numbers: 2, 3, 5, 7, 11, 13, 17, 19, and 23. A **factor** divides evenly into another number. When two or more factors are multiplied together, they equal that number.

In order to find the prime factors of a number, you must factor a number using only prime numbers. When finding prime factors, start with 2, then 3, then 5, and so on, until the number is expressed completely by prime factors.

Examples:
6 = 2 x 3
8 = 2 x 2 x 2
9 = 3 x 3
10 = 2 x 5
12 = 2 x 2 x 3
22 = 2 x 11
27 = 3 x 3 x 3
35 = 5 x 7
39 = 3 x 13
42 = 2 x 3 x 7

UNIT 2

1. EXPONENTS

Definition: An **exponent** on a number means raise it to a power.

Positive Exponents

$$2^2 = 2 \times 2 = 4$$

$$2^3 = 2 \times 2 \times 2 = 8$$

$$2^4 = 2 \times 2 \times 2 \times 2 = 16$$

Negative Exponents

$$2^{-2} = \frac{2^{-2}}{1} = \frac{1}{2^2} = \frac{1}{2} \times \frac{1}{2} = \frac{1}{4}$$

$$2^{-3} = \frac{2^{-3}}{1} = \frac{1}{2^3} = \frac{1}{2} \times \frac{1}{2} \times \frac{1}{2} = \frac{1}{8}$$

A negative exponent means a reciprocal. A reciprocal is one divided by that number. Notice that when a number with a negative exponent goes from the numerator to the denominator, the exponent turns positive.

2. THE FIRST LAW OF EXPONENTS

When multiplying numbers with the same base, you add the exponents.

$$x^m \times x^n = x^{m+n}$$
$$x^2 \times x^3 = x^{2+3} = x^5$$
$$x^2 \times x^{-5} = x^{2-5} = x^{-3}$$

$$4^5 \times 4^2 = 4^7$$
$$5^3 \times 5^6 = 5^9$$
$$8^4 \times 8^2 = 8^6$$

3.   THE SECOND LAW OF EXPONENTS

When dividing numbers with the same base, you subtract the bottom exponent from the top exponent.

$$\frac{x^m}{x^n} = x^{m-n}$$

$$\frac{x^5}{x^2} = x^{5-2} = x^3$$

$$\frac{x^8}{x^{-3}} = x^{8--3} = x^{8+3} = x^{11}$$

4.   MULTIPLYING AND DIVIDING MONOMIALS

Examples:

$$x^2 \times x^3 = x \times x \times x \times x \times x = x^5$$

$$x \times x^6 = x^1 \times x^6 = x \times x \times x \times x \times x \times x \times x = x^7$$

$$\frac{x^3}{x^2} = \frac{\cancel{x} \times \cancel{x} \times x}{\cancel{x} \times \cancel{x}} = x$$

$$\frac{x^2 y^3}{xy} = \frac{\cancel{x} \times x \times \cancel{y} \times y \times y}{\cancel{x} \times y} = xy^2$$

$$(4^5)^2 = (4^5)(4^5) = (4 \times 4 \times 4 \times 4 \times 4)(4 \times 4 \times 4 \times 4 \times 4) = 4^{10}$$

$$(2^3)^3 = (2^3)(2^3)(2^3) = (2 \times 2 \times 2)(2 \times 2 \times 2)(2 \times 2 \times 2) = 2^9$$

$$(5^2)^4 = (5^2)(5^2)(5^2)(5^2) = (5 \times 5)(5 \times 5)(5 \times 5)(5 \times 5) = 5^8$$

UNIT 3

1.   SCIENTIFIC NOTATION

The purpose of scientific notation is to use only a few numbers in order to represent a number with a lot of zeros. But sometimes you want to see the entire number in decimal form.

Task: Change the following numbers from scientific notation into decimal form.

A **positive exponent** means moving the decimal point that many places to *the right*, and then adding zeros in the open places.

$2.5 \times 10^2 =$ 2.5 0   = 250

$2.5 \times 10^3 =$ 2.5 0 0   = 2,500

A **negative exponent** means moving the decimal point that many places to *the left*, and then adding zeros in the open places.

$$2.5 \times 10^{-2} = \quad 0 \; 2.5 \quad = 0.025$$

$$2.5 \times 10^{-3} = \quad 0 \; 0 \; 2.5 \quad = 0.0025$$

2.   THE SQUARE ROOT OF A NUMBER

Squaring a number and taking the **square root of a number** are opposite operations. Squaring a number means multiplying a number times itself. Taking the square root means find a number that, when multiplied times itself, equals the original number. For example, 5 squared equals 25, while the square root of 25 equals 5.

Question: A whole number is squared and the result is between 100 and 225.

The number must be between which two numbers?

Answer: This question is really asking you to find the square root of 100 and then the square root of 225.

The square root of 100 is 10 because 10 x 10 = 100.

The square root of 225 is 15 because 15 x 15 = 225.

Therefore, the final answer is, "the number must be between 10 and 15."

3. ABSOLUTE VALUE

Questions: What is the absolute value of 4? What is the absolute value of −4?

Note: The absolute value of a number can be represented using symbols. For example:

$$|4| \quad \text{or} \quad |-4|$$

Answers: Both equal 4. The absolute value of a number is always positive.

$$|4| = 4$$

$$|-4| = 4$$

4. ADDING POSITIVE AND NEGATIVE NUMBERS

Examples:

$$(5) + (-3) = 2$$
$$(-5) + (6) = 1$$
$$(5) + (-8) = -3$$
$$(-3) + (-2) = -5$$

Using the Number Line: You can use the number line to help you add positive and negative numbers together.

Important Note: Another thing to remember is that subtracting a negative number means add. For example, 1 − −4 equals 1 + 4 = 5.

CAHSEE

Part 2:

Measurement and Geometry

MEASUREMENT & GEOMETRY

2

UNIT 4

1. MEASUREMENT

Question: There are 5,280 feet in one mile. How many feet are there in $1\frac{1}{2}$ miles?

Answer: Multiply 5,280 times 1.5

$$
\begin{array}{r}
5,280 \\
\times\,1.5 \\
\hline
2640.0 \\
5280.0 \\
\hline
7,920 \quad \text{feet}
\end{array}
$$

2. MAKING A SCALED DRAWING

Given: Assume that each unit of measurement on the graph below represents one foot.

Task: Draw a flowerbed that is the shape of a rectangle with the measurements of 3 feet by 4 feet. *Question:* What is its area?

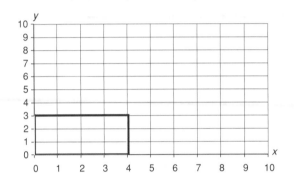

Answer: 3 feet times 4 feet equals 12 square feet

3. READING A SCALED DRAWING

The drawing shown below is a scaled drawing of a Soccer Field where 1 centimeter (cm) = 10 meters.

Question: What is the area of the <u>Penalty Area</u> in square meters?

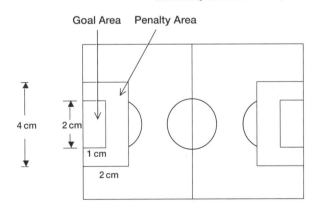

Answer:

<u>First</u>, calculate the large area that includes both the Penalty Area and the Goal Area.

4 cm represents 40 meters, and 2 cm represents 20 meters.

40 x 20 = 800 square meters.

<u>Second</u>, calculate the area of the Goal Area.

2 centimeters represents 20 meters, and 1 cm represents 10 meters.

20 x 10 = 200 square meters.

<u>Lastly</u>, in order to find the Penalty Area, subtract the smaller area from the larger area.

800 – 200 = 600 square meters.

4.   CONVERTING UNITS OF MEASUREMENT

Question: One inch is approximately equal to 2.54 centimeters. Approximately how many centimeters are there in 5 inches?

Answer: Multiply 2.54 x 5 = 12.7 centimeters

Question: One cubic inch is approximately equal to 16.38 cubic centimeters. Approximately how many cubic centimeters are there in 5 cubic inches?

Answer: Multiply 16.38 x 5 = 81.9 cubic centimeters

5. WORD PROBLEM

Question: A car is traveling at the rate of 50 miles per hour. How many minutes will it take to travel 255 miles?

Answer: Start with the formula distance equals rate times time. Then, solve for time. Using this new formula, calculate time by dividing distance by rate. Lastly, convert these hours into minutes by multiplying by 60.

$$\text{Distance} = \text{Rate} \times \text{Time}$$

$$\frac{\text{Distance}}{\text{Rate}} = \text{Time}$$

```
         5.1
     ┌────────
  50 │ 255.0
       250
        50
        50
         0
```

```
    60      minutes
   ×5.1     hours
   ────
    6.0
  300.0
  ─────
   306     minutes
```

UNIT 5

1.   FINDING THE PERIMETER OF A RECTANGLE

Question: What is the perimeter of the following rectangle?

Answer: A perimeter is the distance around an object. 5 + 4 + 5 + 4 = 18 feet

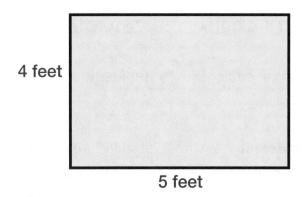

4 feet

5 feet

2.   FINDING THE AREA OF A TRIANGLE

Question: What is the area of this triangle?

Answer: The area of a triangle equals one-half its base times its height.

$$area = \frac{1}{2}bh$$

$$area = \frac{1}{2}(6)(4) = 12 \text{ inches}$$

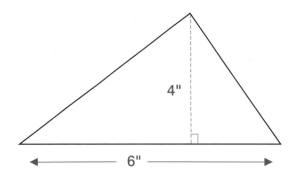

3.   FINDING THE CIRCUMFERENCE AROUND A CIRCLE

Question: Given a circle with a radius of 3 inches, what is its circumference?

Answer: **Circumference** is the distance around a circle. Use the formula, circumference equals 2 times pi times *r*. Pi is (approximately) equal to 3.14, while *r* is the radius of a circle. Remember that the **radius** is the distance from the center out to the circle, while the **diameter** is the distance all the way across and through the center. *Important Note:* An alternative formula for the circumference of a circle is pi times the diameter. This is true because 2 times the radius equals the diameter.

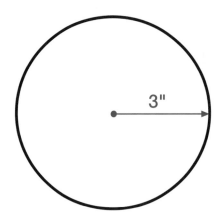

circumference = 2πr
$$= 2(3.14)3$$
$$= 18.84 \text{ inches}$$

4. FINDING THE AREA OF A CIRCLE

Question: What is the area of the circle above?

Area of a circle = πr^2
$$= 3.14 \times (3)^2$$
$$= 3.14 \times 9$$
$$= 28.26 \text{ square inches}$$

Answer: Use the formula, area equals pi times *r* squared.

Given: A circle with a diameter of 12 inches

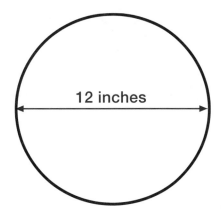

12 inches

Question: What is the area of the circle shown above?

Answer: Use the formula for the area of a circle.

$$(A = \pi r^2 \text{ and } \pi \approx 3.14)$$

Important Note: The formula for the area of a circle uses *r* which is the **radius** of a circle. However, in this problem you are given *d* the

diameter of a circle. Therefore, simply divide the diameter by 2, and you will have the value of the radius. In this problem, 12 divided by 2 is 6. The radius is 6 inches in length.

$$\text{area of a circle} = \pi r^2$$
$$= 3.14 \times (6)^2$$
$$= 3.14 \times 36$$
$$= 113.04 \text{ square inches}$$

5.   FINDING THE AREA OF A COMPLEX FIGURE

Question: What is the area of the figure below?

Answer: Breakup the figure into parts. Compute the area of these parts. Finally, add these areas together.

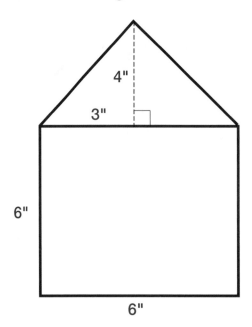

For the square, area equals 6 times 6 which equals 36 square inches. For the triangle, area equals $\frac{1}{2}$ its base times its height. In this case, $\frac{1}{2}(6)(4) = 12$ square inches.

The total area equals 36 + 12 = 48 square inches.

6. FINDING VOLUME

Length is a one-dimensional measurement. Area is a two-dimensional measurement. Volume is a three-dimensional measurement.

Question: What is the volume of the box below?

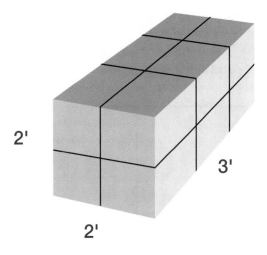

Answer: Multiply **height** times **width** times **length**.

2 × 2 × 3 = 12 cubic feet

7. MORE CONVERTING UNITS OF MEASUREMENT

Question: How many square inches are there in one square foot?

Answer: Make a drawing. Then multiply length times width. 12 inches times 12 inches equals 144 square inches.

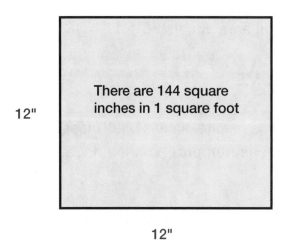

12"

12"

Question: How many square inches are there in the figure below?

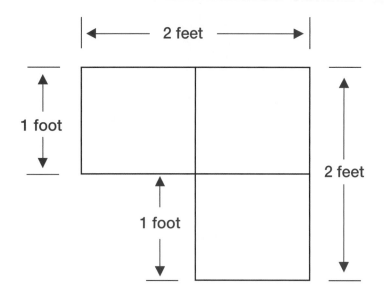

Answer: The figure represents 3 square feet. There are 144 square inches in one square foot. Therefore, the total square inches is 144 times 3, which equals 432 square inches.

UNIT 6

1.   GRAPHING

Task: Plot the following four (*x, y*) coordinates on the graph below: (2, 3) (–4, 4) (–5, –2) & (3, –6).

Answer: A coordinate is simply a point on a graph. The first number is the *x* value, and the second number is the *y* value. The point is located where the *x* value and the *y* value intersect each other on the graph.

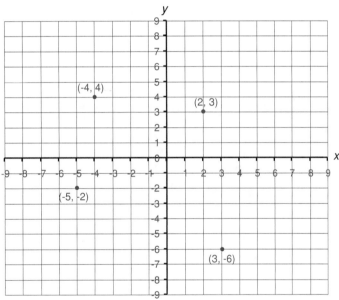

2.   THE PYTHAGOREAN THEOREM

The Pythagorean Theorem tells you about right triangles. A right triangle is a triangle that has a right angle in it. A right angle measures 90 degrees. The Pythagorean Theorem tells you that:

$$a^2 + b^2 = c^2$$

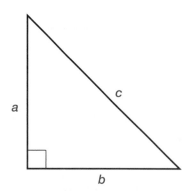

  a and *b* are called legs, and *c* is called the hypotenuse. The hypotenuse is the side of the triangle that is opposite the right angle. The Pythagorean Theorem is useful in the following way: Given the length of any two sides of a right triangle, you can figure out the length of the third.

Question: In a right triangle, one leg is 3 inches the other leg is 4 inches. What is the length of the hypotenuse?

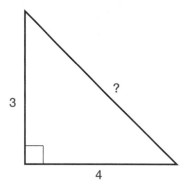

Answer:

$$a^2 + b^2 = c^2$$

$$3^2 + 4^2 = c^2$$

$$9 + 16 = c^2$$

$$25 = c^2$$

$$c = \sqrt{25} = 5 \text{ inches}$$

3. MORE PYTHAGOREAN THEOREM

Question: If one leg of a right triangle is 6 inches, and the hypotenuse is 10 inches, what is the length of the other leg?

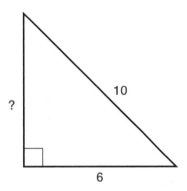

Answer: First, write down the equation for the Pythagorean Theorem. Next, put into the equation whatever information that you are given. The hypotenuse *c* is equal to 10 and one of the legs *b* is equal to 6. Then solve for *a*. Do this by taking 36, changing its sign and then bringing it to the other side of the equal sign. Subtract 36 from 100, which leaves you with 64. Now you have *a* squared, but you want just *a*, so take the square root of each side.

$$a^2 + b^2 = c^2$$

$$a^2 + 6^2 = 10^2$$

$$a^2 + 36 = 100$$

$$a^2 = 100 - 36$$

$$a^2 = 64$$

$$a = \sqrt{64} = 8 \text{ inches}$$

4.   CONGRUENT TRIANGLES

In the same way that numbers are equal, triangles are congruent. You can show that two triangles are congruent in three different ways.

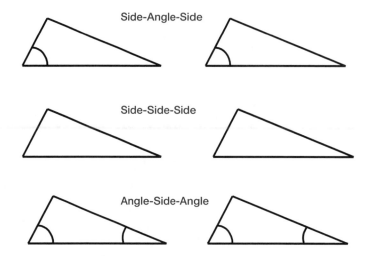

Question: Are these two triangles congruent?

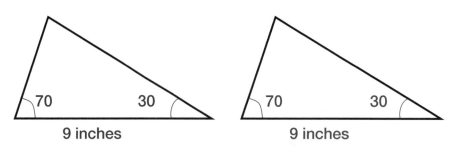

Answer: Yes, because they have two pairs of angles with the same number of degrees, and an included side with the same length.

5.   DEGREES IN A TRIANGLE

The angles of any triangle add up to 180 degrees.

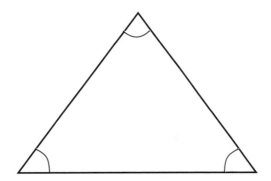

Question: In the triangle below, how many degrees is the missing angle?

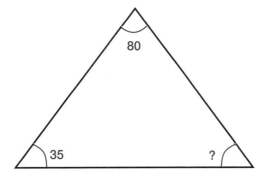

Answer:

$$35 + 80 = 115 \qquad 180 - 115 = 65 \text{ degrees}$$

6.   REFLECTING AN IMAGE ACROSS THE X OR Y AXIS

Task: Draw a triangle *A′ B′ C′* that is the image of triangle *ABC* that results from reflecting the triangle *ABC* across the *x*-axis?

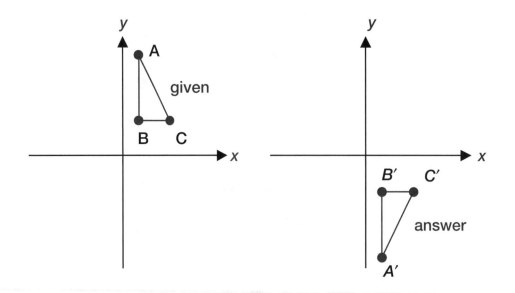

Task: Draw a triangle *A′ B′ C′* that is the image of triangle *ABC* that results from reflecting the triangle *ABC* across the *y*-axis?

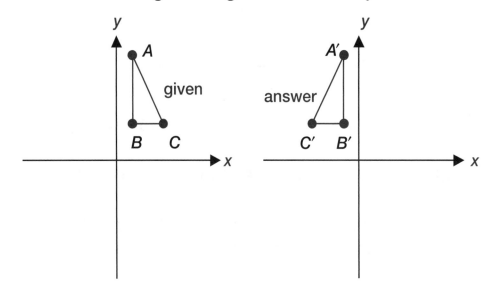

CAHSEE

Part 3:

Statistics, Data Analysis & Probability

STATISTICS, DATA ANALYSIS & PROBABILITY

UNIT 7

1. STATISTICS

The **mean** is the average score. In order to calculate the mean of a set of scores, add up all of the scores and then divide by the number of scores.

The **median** is the score in the middle. First, rank order the scores from smallest to largest. If you have an odd number of scores, then the middle score is the median. If you have an even number of scores, then add the two middle scores and divide by 2. The median score is at the 50th percentile, in other words, it is higher than 50% of all the scores.

The **mode** is the most frequently occurring score.

Questions: Given the set of scores below, what is the mean? What is the median? What is the mode?

Scores: **{3, 2, 5, 6, 2, 2, 1, 3}**

The sum of the 8 scores equals 24.

Answers: If the scores are not already ranked ordered from smallest to largest values, then do this first.

Ranked Ordered Scores: {1, 2, 2, 2, 3, 3, 5, 6}

median
2.5

$$\text{mean} = \frac{24}{8} = 3$$

$$\text{median} = \frac{2+3}{2} = 2.5$$

$$\text{mode} = 2$$

2. PROBABILITY

A **probability** expresses the chances or the likelihood that something happens. This something is called an **outcome**. A probability is a number between 0 and 1 that can be expressed in decimal form. It can also be expressed as a percentage from 0% to 100%. It can also be expressed as a fraction, for example 1/2. If something has a probability of 0, it never happens. If something has a probability of 1, it happens every time. If something has a probability of 0.5, it happens about one-half of the time. If the weatherperson on the TV news says that there is a 60% chance that it will rain tomorrow, there is a 40% chance that it won't. The two probabilities add up to 100%.

Question: If you flip a coin and throw a single die, what is the probability of each outcome?

Answer: The first step is to determine the total number of possible outcomes from this experiment. Since a coin has 2 sides, and a die has 6 sides, there are a total of 12 different possible outcomes from this experiment.

(1 H)	(1 T)
(2 H)	(2 T)
(3 H)	(3 T)
(4 H)	(4 T)
(5 H)	(5 T)
(6 H)	(6 T)

Each outcome has a one out of twelve chance of occurring. The probability of each outcome is 1/12. This fraction can be converted into a decimal and a percentage in the following way:

$$\frac{1}{12} = 12\overline{)1.000} \quad \begin{array}{r} .083 \\ \hline \end{array}$$

$$\begin{array}{r} 96 \\ \hline 40 \\ 36 \\ \hline 4 \end{array}$$

$$\frac{1}{12} \approx 0.08 \text{ or } 8\%$$

Important Definition: An **event** can be a single outcome or a collection of outcomes. For example, you may want to know the probability of the event that the die rolls 4 or 5 and the coin lands heads. In this case, you would simply add the probability of the individual outcomes, 1/12 + 1/12 = 2/12 or 1/6.

UNIT 8

1.   INDEPENDENT AND DEPENDENT EVENTS

Two events are said to be **independent** if the occurrence of one event does not alter the probability that the other event will occur.

Question: Suppose that you flip a fair coin 10 times. And suppose that each time it comes up tails. On the next flip of the coin, what do think the probability is that the coin will land heads?

Answer: 50%, because each flip of a fair coin is independent. In other words, the coin does not remember.

The opposite of independent is dependent. Two events are said to be **dependent** if the occurrence of one event changes the probability that another event occurs.

Question: Is the probability of getting in an automobile accident dependent upon whether the driver has been drinking alcohol or not?

Answer: Yes, they are dependent events. Drinking alcohol increases the probability of getting into an accident.

2.　SCATTERPLOT

A scatterplot is a graph that shows the relationship between two variables. A scatterplot is just a set of (*x, y*) coordinates. Each coordinate is a point on the graph. The *x* value represents a measurement on one variable, while the *y* value represents a measurement on another variable. Remember that a variable is just a measurement that can take on more than one value. A scatterplot is useful because in one picture you can see if there is a relationship between two variables. You've heard the expression, "A picture is worth a thousand words." Likewise, "A graph is worth a thousand numbers."

Given: Variable *x* is Grade Level. Variable *y* is Hours of Homework Each Week.

Task: Using the data below, construct a scatter-plot.

Question: What is the relationship between these two variables?

x Grade Level	1	2	3	4	5	6	7	8	9	10	11	12
y Hours of Homework	2	3	3	6	4	10	7	10	12	9	14	15

Answer: You can think of these two variables as one set of (*x, y*) coordinates on a graph. Remember, a coordinate is just a point. Graph the following points: (1, 2), (2, 3), (3, 3), (4, 6), (5, 4), (6, 10), (7, 7), (8, 10), (9, 12), (10, 9), (11, 14), and (12, 15). This graph shows that as grade level increases, the number of homework hours tends to increase.

Scatterplot

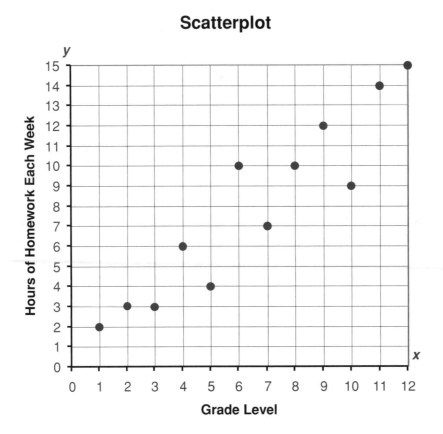

3. CORRELATION

A statistic called correlation tells you if two measurements go together along a straight line. A scatterplot is one way of looking at correlation. There are three different types of correlation.

Positive Correlation. In a positive correlation, as one measurement increases, the other measurement increases.

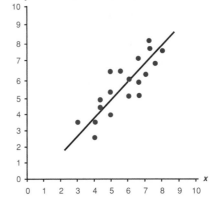

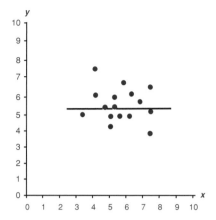

Zero Correlation. In a zero correlation, the two measurements are not related to each other along a straight line.

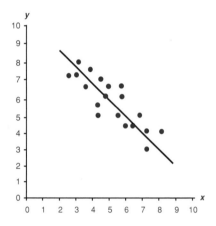

Negative Correlation. In a negative correlation, as one measurement increases, the other measurement decreases.

CAHSEE

Part 4:

Algebra and Functions

ALGEBRA & FUNCTIONS

UNIT 9

1. ALGEBRA BASICS

Multiplying Positive and Negative Numbers:

Words	Symbols	Example
A positive times a positive is a positive.	$(+)(+) = +$	$2(2) = 4$
A positive times a negative is a negative.	$(+)(-) = -$	$2(-2) = -4$
A negative times a positive is a negative.	$(-)(+) = -$	$-2(2) = -4$
A negative times a negative is a positive.	$(-)(-) = +$	$-2(-2) = 4$

Inequalities:

$<$ means *less than*

> means *greater than*

The arrow always points to the smaller number. For example, 5 > 4, –2 < 1, and 0 > –6.

Tips for Word Problems: After reading a word problem try to take out the important information. Write the word, "GIVEN" and next to it write any important numbers from the question. Next, write the word "FIND" and in few words tell what the question wants you to find.

2.   MULTIPLYING TWO BINOMIALS

You multiply two binomials together by using the **FOIL** method. **FOIL** stands for **F**irst, **O**uter, **I**nner, **L**ast. This tells you the order in which to multiply each letter or number. Then combine like terms.

Task: Multiply the following two binomials: $(x + 2)(x + 3)$

Solution:

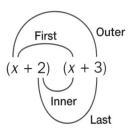

Example: $(x + 2)(x + 3) = x^2 + 3x + 2x + 6$
$$= x^2 + 5x + 6$$
Example: $(2x + 5)(3x - 2) = 6x^2 - 4x + 15x - 10$
$$= 6x^2 + 11x - 10$$

3.　SOLVING AN EQUATION WITH ONE VARIABLE

Think of an equation as a teeter-totter that is balanced in the middle at the = sign. The equation stays balanced just as long as whatever you do to one side, you do to the other side as well. Solving an equation just means to get a variable by itself on one side of the equal sign. In an equation where the variable is x, "solve for x" just means to get x by itself. In order to get x by itself, sometimes you have to add or subtract a number from both sides of the equation. Adding or subtracting a number from both sides of an equation is the same as taking that number, moving it to the other side of the equation, and then changing its sign. In order to get x by itself, sometimes you have to multiply or divide both sides of an equation by a number.

Question: Given the equation $8x + 7 = 47$. Solve for x.

Answer:

$$8x + 7 = 47$$
$$8x = 47 - 7$$
$$8x = 40$$
$$\frac{8x}{8} = \frac{40}{8}$$
$$x = 5$$

4.　SOLVING AN EQUATION WITH TWO VARIABLES

Sometimes an equation has two variables, for example x and y. When an equation has two variables, you can solve for one of them.

Questions: Given the equation $2x + 3y = 12$. Solve for x. Solve for y.

Solving for x: As needed, use addition, subtraction, multiplication, or division in order to get x by itself. The first step in solving this equation is to subtract $3y$ from both sides. Then, divide both sides of the equation by 2.

Solving for x, in other words, getting x by itself.

$$2x + 3y = 12$$
$$2x = -3y + 12$$
$$\frac{2x}{2} = \frac{-3y}{2} + \frac{12}{2}$$
$$x = \frac{-3}{2}y + 6$$

Solving for y: As needed, use addition, subtraction, multiplication, or division in order to get y by itself. The first step in solving this equation is to subtract $2x$ from both sides. Then, divide both sides of the equation by 3.

Solving for y, in other words, getting y by itself.

$$2x + 3y = 12$$
$$3y = -2x + 12$$
$$\frac{3y}{3} = \frac{-2x}{3} + \frac{12}{3}$$
$$y = \frac{-2}{3}x + 4$$

5. SOLVING AN INEQUALITY

Solving an inequality is very much like solving an equation. The basic idea is to get *x* (or whatever variable you are given) by itself. The only difference with inequalities is that if you multiply or divide by a negative number, then you change the direction of the inequality.

Question: Solve for *x* in the following inequality: $2x + 3 < 11$

Answer:

$$2x + 3 < 11$$
$$2x < 11 - 3$$
$$2x < 8$$
$$\frac{2x}{2} < \frac{8}{2}$$
$$x < 4$$

Question: Solve for *x* in the following inequality: $-5x + 2 > 12$

Answer:

$$-5x + 2 > 12$$
$$-5x > 12 - 2$$
$$-5x > 10$$
$$\frac{-5x}{-5} < \frac{10}{-5}$$
$$x < -2$$

6. ESTIMATION

Estimation means coming up with an answer that is close to an exact answer. The advantage of estimation is that it saves you time. Estimates are obtained by rounding off numbers and then performing simple calculations.

Question: Jim is having a pizza party for 11 of his close friends. He wants to serve each guest a mini-pizza. Mini-pizzas cost $6.79 each. Estimate the total cost.

Answer: Round off 11 to 10. Round off $6.79 to $7.00. Then Multiply $7 times 10 which equals $70.

Note: The actual price is $74.36.

7. EVALUATING AN EQUATION

Evaluating an equation means substituting the numbers in for the letters and then simplifying.

Question: If *x* = 4 and *y* = 6, what does the following equation equal?

$$\frac{xy + 3}{9} = \frac{(4)(6) + 3}{9}$$
$$= \frac{24 + 3}{9}$$
$$= \frac{27}{9}$$
$$= 3$$

UNIT 10

1. EXPRESSIONS AND EQUATIONS

Algebra is a language. Speaking algebra involves translating written English into algebraic expressions or equations. "Less than" means "subtract." "More" means "add." "Is" means "equals." "Of" means "times." After reading a word problem once, read it again substituting in the word **equals** for the word "is" and the word **times** for the word "of."

English Words	Algebra
three less than a number	$x - 3$
half as large as area A	$A/2$
five more than twice a number	$2x + 5$
one less than 5 times a number is 14	$5x - 1 = 14$
25% of a number	$0.25x$

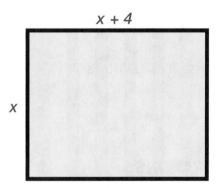

$x + 4$

x

Question: The length of the rectangle above is 4 units longer than the width. What expression represents the area of the rectangle?

Answer: Multiply the width times the length

$$x(x + 4) = x^2 + 4x$$

2. GROUPING SYMBOLS

Parentheses **( )** and brackets **[ ]** are grouping symbols. Parentheses and brackets mean, "Do this first." If there are parentheses inside of brackets, then do what is in the parentheses first. Work from the inside out. When a number is next to parentheses or a bracket, this means multiply.

Question: What does $5(2 + 4)$ equal?

Answer: $5(2 + 4) = 5(6) = 30$

Question: What does $-3(8 \div 2)$ equal?

Answer: $-3(8 \div 2) = -3(4) = -12$

Question: What does $5(x + 2)$ equal?

Answer: $5(x + 2) = 5x + 10$

Question: What does $4(x - 1)$ equal?

Answer: $4(x - 1) = 4x - 4$

3. ORDER OF OPERATIONS

When an expression does not have grouping symbols, you must follow the **Order of Operations.** This rule tells you to do powers first, multiplication and division second, and addition and subtraction third. These operations are carried out from left to right.

Example: $4 + 8 \div 2 = 4 + (8 \div 2) = 4 + 4 = 8$

Example: $4 - 5 \times 3 = 4 - (5 \times 3) = 4 - 15 = -11$

Example: $3 \times 2^3 = 3 \times 8 = 24$

Example: $3(2 + 5)^2 = 3[(2x + 5)(2x + 5)]$

$$= 3[4x^2 + 10x + 10x + 25]$$

$$= 3[4x^2 + 20x + 25]$$

$$= 12x^2 + 60x + 75$$

UNIT 11

1. READING A BAR GRAPH

Given: The bar graph below is for the fictitious city of Greenville. The measurement on the *x*-axis is month of the year. The measurement on the *y*-axis is average monthly rainfall.

Questions: Which month has the third-lowest average rainfall? What is this measurement in inches?

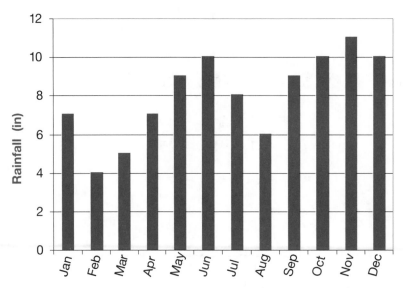

Average Monthly Rainfall for the City of Greenville

Answers: August has the third-lowest average rainfall. August has an average of 6 inches of rain.

2. PERCENT SAVINGS

Question: Blue Jeans regularly sell for $40. This week they are on sale for $32. What is the percent savings?

Answer: First, subtract the sale price from the regular price. Second, divide the amount saved by the regular price. Lastly, change this decimal into a percent.

$$40 - 32 = 8$$

$$\frac{8}{40} = 40\overline{)8.0}$$

$$0.2 = 20\%$$

3. SALE PRICE

Question: Music CDs are regularly $20 each. But this week only, they are on sale for 15% off. How much is the sale price?

Answer: First, find out how much money is saved. Then, subtract this savings from the regular price in order to find the sale price.

$$
\begin{array}{r}
20 \\
\underline{\times 0.15} \\
100 \\
\underline{200} \\
3.00
\end{array}
$$

$20.00 − $3.00 = $17.00

UNIT 12

1. GRAPHING A FUNCTION

Task: Graph the function $y = \dfrac{1}{2}x^2$

Solution: When creating a graph, make two columns and label the first column x and the second column y. Then, under the x column put in the values 0, 1, −1, 3, and −3. Next, calculate the y values for each x value by plugging the x value into the equation. Finally, plot the (x, y) points on the graph and connect the points. *Note:* This curve is called a parabola.

x	y
0	0
1	0.5
−1	0.5
3	4.5
−3	4.5

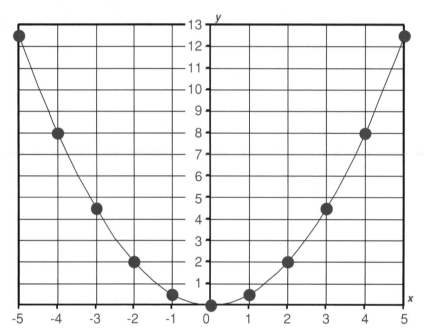

Note: In order to create a more detailed graph of this function, additional *x* values of 2, –2, 4, –4, 5, and –5 were used in the above graph.

2. THE SLOPE OF A LINE

Definition: Slope measures the steepness of a line.

$$\text{Slope} = \frac{\text{rise}}{\text{run}} = \text{the amount of change in } y \text{ for each one}$$

unit change in *x*.

Example: The equation $y = 2x + 3$ is the equation of a line with slope equal to 2. This means that for every one-unit change in *x*, the *y* measurement goes up 2 units. By the way, the number 3 in this equation is called the *y*-intercept. The *y*-intercept is the point where the line crosses the *y*-axis. The *y*-intercept is the value of *y* when *x* equals 0. The general equation for a line is $y = mx + b$ where *m* is the slope and *b* is the *y*-intercept.

$y = 2x + 3$

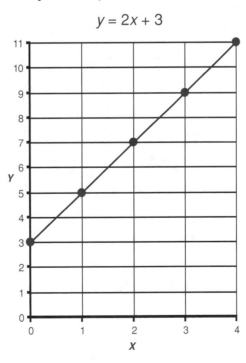

3. READING A LINE GRAPH

A line graph shows the relationship between two measurements, for example between the number of music CDs that someone buys and the total cost.

Question: How much would it cost to buy 4 music CDs?

Answer: Find 4 on the axis labeled "Number of Music CDs." Go straight up until you hit the line, then look left at the axis labeled "Total Cost." The cost is $60.

Question: How much does each CD cost?

Answer: This is actually the slope. By looking at the graph, we can see that for each one-unit change in number of CDs, the total cost goes up $15.

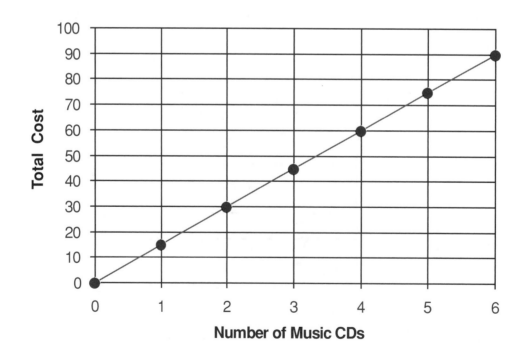

4. MORE READING A LINE GRAPH

Given: The equation and the graph of the line below

Question: What is the slope of this line?

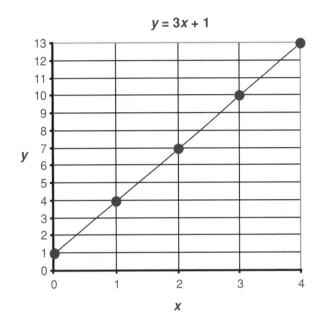

Question: What is the *y*-intercept of this line?

Question: For an *x* value of 5, what would its *y* value be?

Answers: The equation $y = 3x + 1$ is the equation of a line with slope equal to 3. This means that for every one-unit change in *x*, the *y* measurement goes up 3 units.

The *y*-intercept is 1. The *y*-intercept is the point where the line crosses the *y*-axis. The general equation for a line is $y = mx + b$ where *m* is the slope and *b* is the *y*-intercept.

Using the equation $y = 3x + 1$, an *x* value of 5 would give a *y* value of 16 because $y = 3(5) + 1 = 16$.

CAHSEE

Part 5:

Algebra I

ALGEBRA I

UNIT 13

1. SOLVING A LINEAR EQUATION

Given: $-x + 2y = 6$

Task: Solve for y.

Question: If x equals 10, what does y equal?

Solution:　　Solve for y.

$$-x + 2y = 6$$

$$2y = x + 6$$

$$\frac{2y}{2} = \frac{x}{2} + \frac{6}{2}$$

$$y = \frac{x}{2} + 3$$

If $x = 10$, what does y equal?

$$y = \frac{10}{2} + 3$$

$$y = 5 + 3 = 8$$

2.   WORD PROBLEM

Question: If a train travels 140 miles in $3\frac{1}{2}$ hours, what is its average rate of speed?

Answer: Use the formula "distance equals rate times time."

$$D = R \times T$$

Solve for R by dividing both sides of the equation by T.

$$\frac{D}{T} = \frac{R \times \cancel{T}}{\cancel{T}}$$

$$\frac{D}{T} = R = \frac{140 \text{ miles}}{3.5 \text{ hours}} = 40 \text{ miles per hour}$$

The average rate of speed is 40 miles per hour.

3. OPPOSITES AND RECIPROCALS

Definition: When a number is added to its **opposite**, it equals 0. To find the opposite of a number, just change the sign of the number.

Examples: The opposite of 5 is –5. The opposite of –8 is 8.

Definition: The **reciprocal** of a number is that number's fraction turned upside down.

Question: Find the reciprocal of 2.

Answer: $2 = \dfrac{2}{1}$, so the reciprocal of 2 equals $\dfrac{1}{2}$.

Question: Find the reciprocal of $\dfrac{4}{7}$.

Answer: The reciprocal of $\dfrac{4}{7}$ equals $\dfrac{7}{4}$.

Note: A number multiplied by its reciprocal always equals 1.

Question: If $x = -6$, what does $-x$ equal?

Answer: If $x = -6$, then $-x = -(-6) = 6$.

Note: The opposite of a negative number is a positive number.

UNIT 14

1.   MORE ABSOLUTE VALUE

Definition: An **absolute value** is the positive value of a number. The absolute value of any number is always positive.

Example: |6| = 6 |–6| = 6

Solve: |x – 2| = 5

Answer: This means that either

x – 2 = 5   or   x – 2 = –5.
x = 5 + 2   or   x = –5 + 2
x = 7   or   x = –3

Final answer: {7, –3}

2.   MORE ABOUT SOLVING A LINEAR EQUATION

Question: What does *x* equal in the following equation?

3(2x – 5) + 4(x – 2) = 12

Answer: Solve for *x*. In other words, get *x* by itself.

$3(2x - 5) + 4(x - 2) = 12$ Get rid of the parenthesis by distributing

$6X - 15 + 4x - 8 = 12$ Combine like terms

$10x - 23 = 12$ Bring the -23 over to the other side

and change its sign

$10x = 12 + 23$ Add 12 and 23

$10x = 35$ Divide both sides by 10

$$\frac{10x}{10} = \frac{35}{10}$$

$$X = \frac{35}{10}$$

$x = 3.5$

Note: When dividing by 10 or 100 or 1000, and so on, just move the decimal point of the numerator to the left, one space for each 0.

3.   WORD PROBLEM

Question: Britney went to the County Fair and spent a total of $27. She spent $6 on admission, $9 on food, and went on 8 rides. All of the rides were the same price. What was the price of each ride?

Answer: Turn this word problem into an equation and then solve for the missing value.

$$6 + 9 + 8x = 27$$
$$15 + 8x = 27$$
$$8x = 27 - 15$$
$$8x = 12$$
$$x = \frac{12}{8}$$

```
     1.5
 8)12.0
     8.0
     4.0
     4.0
       0
```

Final Answer: Each ride cost $1.50.

UNIT 15

1.   GRAPHING A LINE

Questions: You are given the equation $6x + 2y = 4$. What is the slope of this line? What is the *y*-intercept of this line? What does a graph of this line look like?

Solutions: In order to find the slope and the *y*-intercept, you must solve for *y*.

$$6x + 2y = 4$$

$$2y = -6x + 4$$

$$\frac{2y}{2} = \frac{-6x}{2} + \frac{4}{2}$$

$$y = -3x + 2$$

Once you have solved for *y*, reading the slope and the *y*-intercept are easy. The slope is the number that is being multiplied times *x*. The *y*-intercept is the number that is being added to or subtracted from the *x* term. In the equation $y = -3x + 2$, the slope is –3 and the *y*-intercept is 2. The general equation for a line is $y = mx + b$ where *m* is the slope and *b* is the *y*-intercept.

To graph a line you really only need two points. The *y*-intercept (0, 2) is a good point. A second point can be found by letting *x* equal any value and then solving for *y*. For example, when *x* equals 3, $y = -3(3) + 2 = -7$. So the point (3, –7) falls on this line. Plot these two points (0, 2) and (3, –7) and connect them by a line. In the graph below, one additional point (–3, 11) was included for greater detail, though it was not necessary.

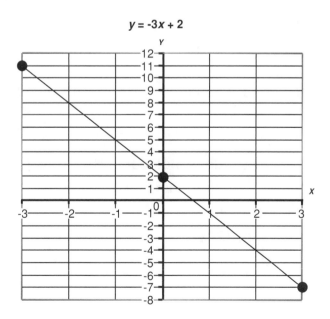

$y = -3x + 2$

2. A POINT ON A LINE

To find out if a point (x, y) falls on a line, you put these (x, y) values into the equation. If the equation is true, then the point falls on the line. If the equation is false, then the point *does not* fall on the line.

Question: Which one of the following points falls on the line expressed by the following equation?

$$2x + 3y = 16$$

(1, 6) (2, 3) (2, 4) (3, 5)

Answer: The strategy is to plug each point into the equation, one at a time, until you find a point that makes the equation true.

$2(1) + 3(6) = 20$ 20 does not equal 16. This point does not fall on the line.

$2(2) + 3(3) = 13$ 13 does not equal 16. This point does not fall on the line.

$2(2) + 3(4) = 16$ 16 equals 16. True. *This point falls on the line.*

$2(3) + 3(5) = 21$ 21 does not equal 16. This point does not fall on the line.

Final Answer: The point (2, 4) falls on the line expressed by the equation $2x + 3y = 16$.

3. COORDINATES OF X- AND Y-INTERCEPTS

Question: What are the coordinates of the *x*-intercept of the following line?

$$3x - 2y = 12$$

Answer: This question is asking "What is the value of *x* when *y* equals 0?"

In order to answer this question, substitute 0 in for *y* and solve for *x*.

$$3x - 2(0) = 12$$

$$3x = 12$$

$$\frac{3x}{3} = \frac{12}{3}$$

$$x = 4$$

Final Answer: The coordinates of the *x*-intercept are (4, 0).

Question: What are the coordinates of the *y*-intercept of the following line?

$$3x - 2y = 12$$

Answer: This question is asking "What is the value of *y* when *x* equals 0?"

In order to answer this question, substitute 0 in for *x* and solve for *y*.

$$3(0) - 2y = 12$$

$$-2y = 12$$

$$\frac{-2y}{-2} = \frac{12}{-2}$$

$$y = -6$$

Final Answer: The coordinates of the *y*-intercept are (0, –6).

4.   PARALLEL LINES

Two lines are parallel when their slopes are equal.

Example:

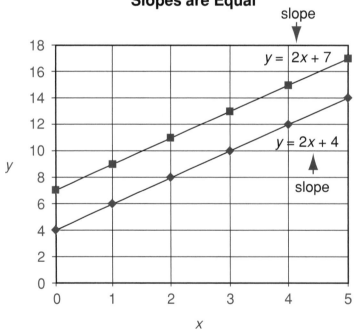

Two Lines are Parallel when their Slopes are Equal

In the above graph, both lines have a slope of 2. The slope is the number that is being multiplied by *x*. Notice that parallel lines have different *y*-intercepts.

UNIT 16

1. SOLVING A SYSTEM OF TWO LINEAR EQUATIONS AND UNDERSTANDING THE SOLUTION GRAPHICALLY

Question: What is the solution to the system of two linear equations stated below?

$$\begin{cases} 2x + y = 8 \\ x - y = 1 \end{cases}$$

Answer: This question is really asking, "Given the equations for two different lines, what value of *x* and *y* fit both equations?" Solve by substitution. First, solve for *x* using one of the equations.

$$x - y = 1, \text{ so} \qquad x = y + 1$$

Then, substitute (*y* + 1) in for *x* in the other equation and solve for *y*.

$$2(y + 1) + y = 8$$

$$2y + 2 + y = 8$$

$$3y + 2 = 8$$

$$3y = 8 - 2$$

$$3y = 6$$

$$\frac{3y}{3} = \frac{6}{3}$$

$$y = 2$$

Next, substitute this *y* value of 2 into either one of the original equations and solve for *x*.

$$x - y = 1$$
$$x - 2 = 1$$
$$x = 1 + 2$$
$$x = 3$$

Final Answer: The solution is *x* = 3 and *y* = 2. In other words, the point (3, 2) fits both equations.

Question: What do the solutions *x* = 3 and *y* = 2 mean graphically?

The Intersection of Two Lines

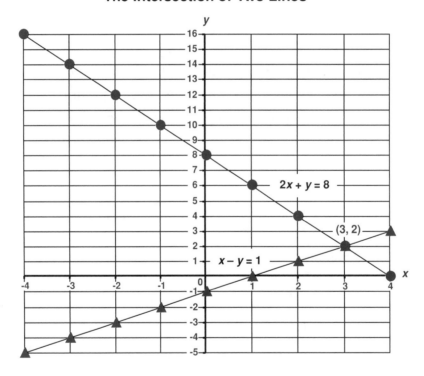

Answer: This means that the two lines intersect at the point (3, 2).

Alternative Method for Finding the Solution to a System of Linear Equations

You learn in mathematics that sometimes it is better to work backwards in order to solve a problem. This is one of those times. Because the CAHSEE in math has a multiple-choice format, it is possible to work this type of problem backwards. It works like this: In the same way that you can take a point (x, y) and put it into the equation of a line to see if it is true, you can do this to two equations. When a point is true for both equations, it is the right answer. That point represents the intersection of the two lines. Because you will have four answers to choose from, *try each of the possible points, one at a time, until you find a point that is true for both equations.* That will be the correct answer.

2. SIMPLIFYING EXPRESSIONS

You simplify expressions by adding like terms together.

Add the terms with x^2 together.

Add the terms with x together.

Add the numbers together.

Examples: Simplify: $2x^2 + 4x + 1 + 3x^2 + 3x + 12$

$$= 5x^2 + 7x + 13$$

Simplify: $-4x + 2 + 5x - 6 = x - 4$

Simplify: $\dfrac{36x^4y^5}{18x^2y} = 2x^{4-2}y^{5-1} = 2x^2y^4$

Simplify: $5x \times 5x^2 = 25x^3$

Simplify: $(4x^3y^2)(9x^5y) = (4xxxyy)(9xxxxxy) = 36x^8y^3$

Simplify: $(3x^7y^2)(7x^4y^2) = (3xxxxxxxyy)(7xxxxyy)$
$$= 21x^{11}y^4$$

Simplify: $(5x^2y^6z^3)(5x^5y^3z^4)$
$$= (5xxyyyyyyzzz)(5xxxxxyyyzzzz)$$
$$= 25x^7y^9z^7$$

3. WORD PROBLEM

Question: A train is traveling at a rate of 40 miles per hour. Its destination is 200 miles away. How long will the trip take?

Answer: Using the formula "distance equals rate times time," solve for time. In other words, get *T* by itself. You get *T* by itself by dividing both sides of the equation by *R*. Lastly, divide the distance of 200 miles by the rate of 40 miles per hour in order to calculate time.

$$D = R \times T$$
$$\frac{D}{R} = \frac{\cancel{R} \times T}{\cancel{R}}$$
$$\frac{D}{R} = T = \frac{200}{40} = 5 \text{ hours}$$

4. FINDING AN EQUIVALENT EQUATION

Given: $\quad \dfrac{5}{x+2} = \dfrac{8}{x}$

Task: Come up with an equation that is equivalent to the equation shown above.

Solution: There are a number of possible solutions to this task. One solution involves eliminating the denominators by cross-multiplying like this:

$$\frac{5}{x+2} = \frac{8}{x}$$

$$\frac{5}{x+2} \diagdown \frac{8}{x}$$

$$5x = 8(x+2)$$

FORMULAS

Distance = Rate × Time

$$\frac{\text{Distance}}{\text{Rate}} = \text{Time}$$

$$\frac{\text{Distance}}{\text{Time}} = \text{Rate}$$

The area of a triangle is $\frac{1}{2}bh$

The circumference of a circle is $2\pi r$ or πd

The area of a circle is πr^2

There are 180° in a triangle

The Pythagorean theorem $a^2 + b^2 = c^2$

CAHSEE

Practice Test 1

Practice Test

1

TIME: Untimed
80 Questions

DIRECTIONS: Give only one answer to each question. If you change an answer, be sure that the previous mark is erased completely.

Notes: (1) Figures that accompany problems are drawn as accurately as possible EXCEPT when it is stated that a figure is not drawn to scale. All figures lie in a plane unless otherwise noted. (2) All numbers used are real numbers. All algebraic expressions represent real numbers unless otherwise stated. *

(Answer sheets are located in the back of this book.)

1. $\dfrac{3}{8} + \dfrac{4}{7} =$

   A $\dfrac{53}{56}$

   B $\dfrac{21}{56}$

   C $\dfrac{7}{15}$

   D $\dfrac{12}{15}$

* Reprinted by permission of California High School Exit Exam (CAHSEE), California Department of Education, P.O. Box 271, Sacramento, CA 95812-0271.

2. $2.4 \times 10^3 =$

   A   2.400

   B   24

   C   240

   D   2,400

3.   **Which of the following equals a negative number?**

   A $(-5) + (9)$

   B $(-9) + (5)$

   C $(9) + (5)$

   D $(5) + (-9) + (4)$

4. $\dfrac{15x^2y^4}{3xy^2} =$

   A $5x^3y$

   B $5xy^6$

   C $5x^3y^6$

   D $5xy^2$

5.   **Music CDs are on sale. The original price was $15.00. The sale price is $12.00. What is the percent saving?**

   A   5%

   B   10%

   C   20%

   D   25%

6. The crew from a fishing boat reports catching fish 90 days out of a total of 190 days of fishing. Estimate the approximate percentage of the time the crew caught fish?

    A   23%

    B   50%

    C   75%

    D   110%

7. $5^3 \times 5^7 =$

    A 5^{10}

    B 5^{21}

    C 25^{10}

    D 25^{21}

8. General admission tickets to a concert hall regularly cost $32.00. They are on sale for 20% off. What is the sale price of the tickets?

    A $22.40

    B $20.50

    C $25.60

    D $30.00

9. A die has six sides. What is the probability of rolling a 2 or a 3 in one throw of a fair die?

    A $\dfrac{1}{6}$

B $\dfrac{1}{3}$

C $\dfrac{1}{2}$

D $\dfrac{2}{3}$

10. **Ten is multiplied by a number between 0 and 1. The answer has to be between which two numbers?**

   A   0 and 10

   B   0 and 100

   C   0 and 10 but not 5

   D   0 and 100 but not 50

11. **Which fraction does 80% equal?**

   A $\dfrac{1}{4}$

   B $\dfrac{1}{3}$

   C $\dfrac{3}{8}$

   D $\dfrac{4}{5}$

12. **On a math quiz, Jim is asked to write down the mathematical expression for the words, "five more than three times a number."**

Jim incorrectly answers *8x*. Which expression should he have used?

A   5*x*

B   5(3*x*)

C   5*x* + 3

D   3*x* + 5

13. A local shoe store is having a sale. All athletic shoes are 15% off. What is the sale price of a pair of shoes that regularly costs $60?

A $42

B $45

C $48

D $51

14. Which of the following is the prime factored form of lowest common denominator of $\frac{5}{6} + \frac{2}{7}$?

A   2 × 3 × 7

B   7 × 1

C   6 × 7

D   2 × 3 × 5

15. **A whole number is squared and the result is between 225 and 400.**

    The number must be between _____ .

    A 5 and 10

    B 10 and 15

    C 15 and 20

    D 20 and 25

16. **The absolute value of –7 is equal to which of the following?**

    A $\dfrac{1}{7}$

    B 7

    C $-\dfrac{1}{7}$

    D –7

17. **When eating at a restaurant, a common practice is to tip the waiter or waitress 15% of the price of the meal. An easy way to calculate the tip is to take 10% of the bill, plus $\dfrac{1}{2}$ of that. Using this rule, if a restaurant bill comes to $16.00, how much should the tip be?**

    A $1.50

    B $2.00

    C $2.40

    D $3.20

18. The winning number in a drawing is less than 60. It is a multiple of 2, 5, and 8. What is the number?

    A   10

    B   16

    C   40

    D   48

19. What is the best estimate of 216 × 192?

    A   400

    B   4,000

    C   40,000

    D   400,000

20. A fair coin is flipped twice. What is the probability of getting two heads?

    A   10%

    B   25%

    C   50%

    D   75%

21. The chart below shows the English test scores of three students.

	Test 1	Test 2	Test 3	Test 4
Peter	10	7	5	4
Paul	3	6	9	10
Mary	9	8	10	5

What is Mary's mean score?

A   7

B   8

C   9

D   10

22.   The graph below represents the high temperature for five days of the week. Which day has the greatest increase in temperature over that of the previous day?

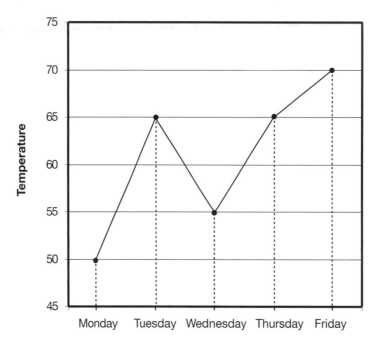

A   Tuesday

B   Wednesday

C   Thursday

D   Friday

23. A weather person on the evening news says that there is a 35% chance that it rains tomorrow. What is the probability that it *does not* rain?

   A   10%

   B   25%

   C   50%

   D   65%

24. Tom flips a coin 10 times, and each time it comes up tails. If he flips the coin one more time, what is the probability that it will come up heads?

   A $\dfrac{1}{5}$

   B $\dfrac{1}{2}$

   C $\dfrac{6}{10}$

   D $\dfrac{9}{10}$

25. What is the mode score for the following set of scores?

   {3, 2, 7, 4, 3, 5, 2, 5, 3, 2, 3, 9}

   A   2

   B   3

   C   5

   D   9

26. **ON TIME delivery company uses the data in the table below to support their claim, "We have one-tenth the number of customer complaints that SPEEDY delivery company has." Why is this claim misleading?**

Delivery Company	Customer Complaints	Months in Business
SPEEDY	100	25
ON TIME	10	2

    A   On average, SPEEDY has more complaints.

    B   The claim should say "one-fourth" of the number of complaints.

    C   The claim should say "one-fifth" of the number of complaints.

    D   On average, ON TIME has more complaints *per month*.

27. **Four cards are shown below: a heart, a diamond, a moon, and a sun. If you randomly select a single card, what is the probability that it is *not* a heart?**

    A   0.25

    B   0.33

    C   0.75

    D   1.25

28. Using the graph shown below, what is the temperature for the third-warmest day of the week?

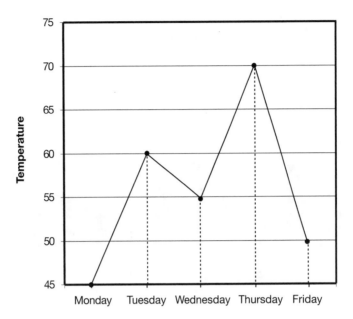

A   50

B   55

C   60

D   70

29. The graph below shows the average monthly rainfall for the city of Batesville. During the month that had the third-smallest amount of rainfall, how many inches did it rain?

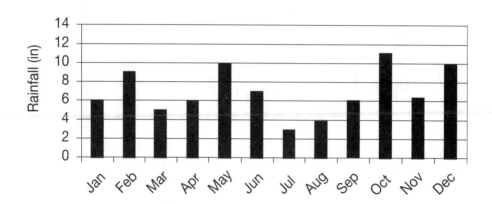

Average Monthly Rainfall for the
City of Batesville

A   3

B   4

C   5

D   6

30. Ashley scores the following amount of points in her high school basketball games: 6, 0, 3, 7, 12, 2, 5. What is her median number of points scored?

A   2

B   5

C   7

D   12

31. The graph below shows the relationship between temperature and sales of jackets in $1000 units. Which statement does this graph support?

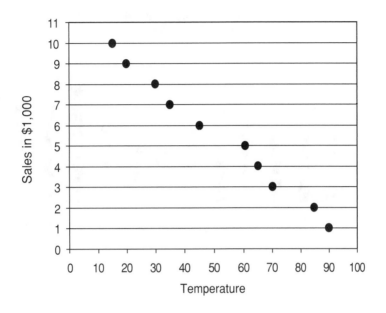

A   As temperature decreases, sales of jackets increase.

B   The sales of jackets are unchanged by temperature.

C   As temperature increases, sales of jackets increase.

D   The sales of jackets are unchanged as temperature increases.

32. The graph below shows the average monthly rainfall for the city of Stuckeyville. Which month has the fourth-highest average monthly rainfall?

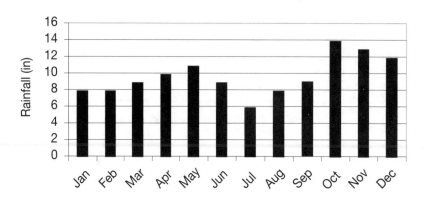

Average Monthly Rainfall for the City of Stuckeyville

A   November

B   April

C   May

D   December

33. Divide a number by 2 and add 3 to the result. The answer is 10.

Which of the following equations expresses these statements?

A $\dfrac{x}{2} + 3 = 10$

B $\dfrac{x}{5} = 10$

C $\quad 3 = \dfrac{x}{2} + 10$

D $\quad \dfrac{x + 3}{2} = 10$

34. **What is the equation of the line shown below?**

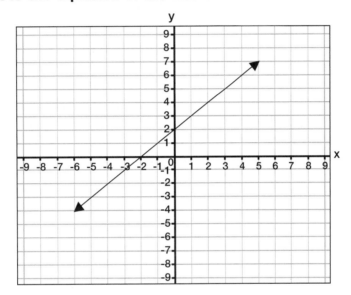

A $\quad y = 2x + 1$

B $\quad y = 2x - 1$

C $\quad y = \dfrac{1}{2}x - 2$

D $\quad y = x + 2$

35. **The scatter plot below shows the relationship between grade level and hours of reading each week. Which statement describes this relationship?**

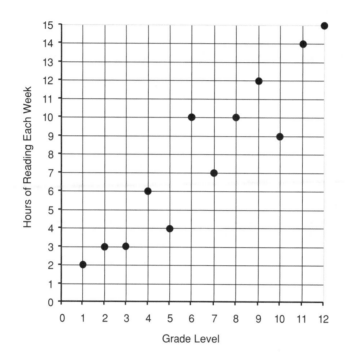

A   As grade level goes down, the number of reading hours goes up.

B   As grade level goes up, the number of reading hours goes down.

C   As grade level goes up, the number of reading hours goes up.

D   Grade level and reading hours are unrelated.

36. **Which of the graphs below could be the graph of $y = x^2$?**

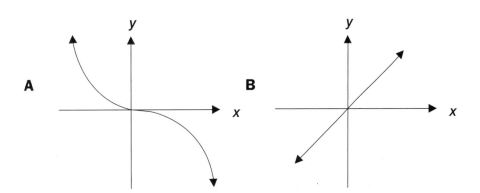

37. **Simplify the following expression: $(3xy^2)(7x^2y^3)$**

A $21x^2y^6$

B $21x^5y^6$

C $21x^3y^5$

D $21x^3y^6$

38. **Solve 3*x* + 5 < 20 for *x*.**

    A   *x* < 3

    B   *x* < 5

    C   *x* < 7

    D   *x* < 9

39. **The graph below shows the interest rate paid by two different banks on a savings account. The interest rate depends upon the amount of the balance.**

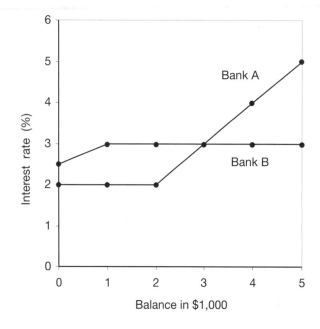

Bank A pays more interest than Bank B for balances of _____.

    A $3,000 only

    B   less than $3,000

    C   more than $3,000

    D   all amounts

40. In a certain class, the number of boys, *b*, is equal to four times the number of girls, *g*. Which of the following equations expresses this sentence?

    A $4 \cdot b = g$

    B $4 \cdot b = g \cdot b$

    C $g \cdot b = 4$

    D $4 \cdot g = b$

41. The graph below shows the relationship between the number of CDs purchased and the total cost. What is the price of each CD?

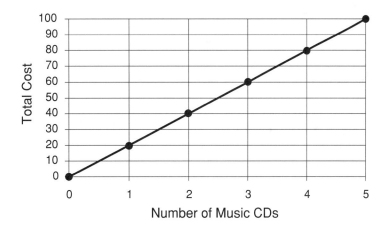

    A $15

    B $20

    C $25

    D $30

42. If $x = 2$ and $y = 5$, then $\dfrac{xy + 4}{3} - 3 =$

    A   4

    B   6

    C   8

    D   10

43. Simplify the following: $(5x^3y^2z)\,(9xy^2z)$

    A $45x^3y^2z$

    B $45x^4y^4z^2$

    C $45x^3y^4z$

    D $45x^4y^4z$

44. Given $4x + 4 = 7$, solve for x.

    A $\dfrac{1}{4}$

    B $\dfrac{1}{2}$

    C $\dfrac{3}{4}$

    D $\dfrac{4}{3}$

45. **What is the slope of the line below?**

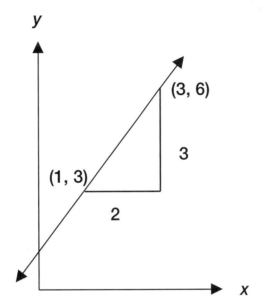

A $-\dfrac{2}{3}$

B $\dfrac{3}{2}$

C $\dfrac{2}{3}$

D $-\dfrac{3}{2}$

46. A gasoline pump pumps gas at the rate of 2.5 gallons a minute. At this rate, how many minutes will it take to fill a car with a gas tank that holds 20 gallons?

    A   6

    B   8

    C   10

    D   12

47. The graph below shows the number of oranges produced by a grower in California for the years 1997, 1999, and 2001.

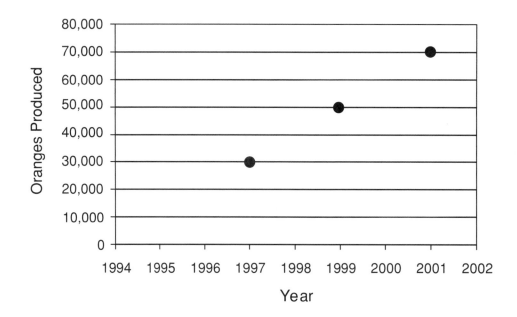

From this graph, which of the following was the most probable number of oranges produced by this grower in 1995?

    A   0

    B   10,000

C   20,000

D   30,000

48. Solve $\dfrac{x}{3} - 2 = 8$ for *x*.

    A   18

    B   21

    C   24

    D   30

49. **What other information is needed in order to solve this problem?**

    A delivery truck made 100 different deliveries in one week and used a total of 40 gallons of gasoline. What was the average number of miles per gallon?

    A   the average number of deliveries made each day

    B   the cost of gasoline per gallon

    C   the average speed per hour

    D   the number of miles traveled

50. **A train travels 376 miles from Los Angeles to San Francisco. The trip takes 8 hours. What is the average speed of the train in miles per hour (mph)?**

    A   41 mph

    B   44 mph

    C   47 mph

    D   50 mph

51. There are approximately 2.54 centimeters in one inch. Approximately how many centimeters are there in 10 inches?

   A   2.5

   B   25

   C   250

   D   2,500

52. What is the value of *x* in the triangle shown below?

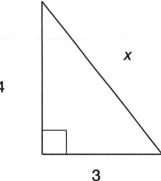

   A   5

   B   6

   C   7

   D   12

53. There are 9 square feet in one square yard. How many square yards are there in 135 square feet?

   A   15

   B   20

   C   25

   D   30

54. **What is the area of the *shaded* region in the figure shown below?**

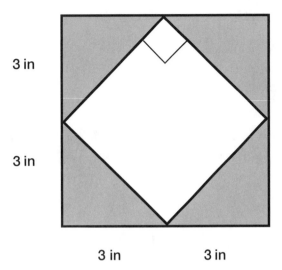

3 in

3 in

3 in   3 in

A   4.5 in²

B   9 in²

C   18 in²

D   32 in²

55. **What is the approximate circumference of the circle shown below?**

($\pi \approx 3.14$)

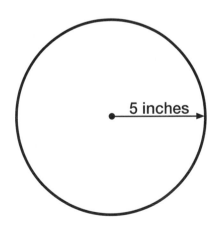

5 inches

A   10 inches

B   16 inches

C   31 inches

D   78 inches

56. **Which of the following triangles A′ B′ C′ is the image of triangle ABC that results from reflecting the triangle ABC across the y-axis?**

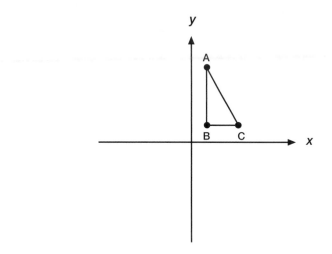

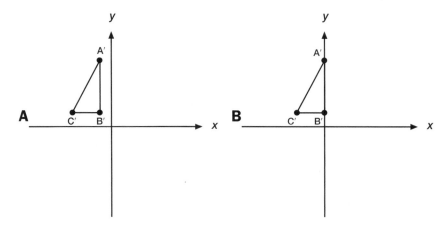

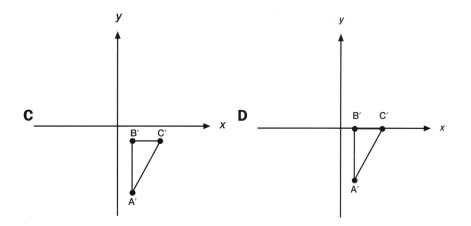

57. **What is the area of the triangle shown below?**

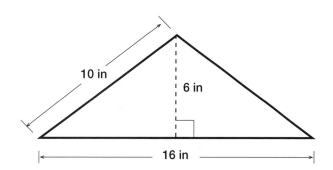

A   24 square inches

B   32 square inches

C   40 square inches

D   48 square inches

58. Approximately how many cubic centimeters are there in 2 cubic inches? (One cubic inch is approximately equal to 16.38 cubic centimeters.)

    A   8.19

    B   18.38

    C   21.38

    D   32.76

59. Two triangles are shown below.

    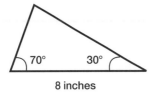 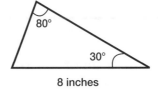

    8 inches   8 inches

    Which of the following statements is true?

    A   The two triangles are congruent.

    B   The two triangles are *not* congruent.

    C   Only one side and one angle are equal.

    D   Both triangles are right triangles.

60. Two triangles are shown below.

    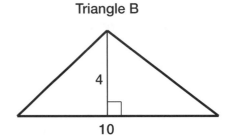

    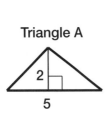

What is $\dfrac{\text{the area of Triangle A}}{\text{the area of Triangle B}}$?

A $\dfrac{1}{8}$

B $\dfrac{1}{4}$

C $\dfrac{1}{2}$

D $\dfrac{3}{4}$

61. **The points (1, 1), (2, 3), (4, 1), (5, 3) are the vertices of a polygon. What type of polygon is formed by these points?**

   A   Triangle

   B   Square

   C   Parallelogram

   D   Trapezoid

62. **The scaled drawing of the tennis court shown below is drawn using the scale 1 inch equals 24 feet.**

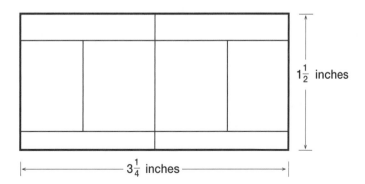

$1\frac{1}{2}$ inches

$3\frac{1}{4}$ inches

What is the length in feet of the tennis court?

A   66 feet

B   78 feet

C   80 feet

D   92 feet

63.   **What is the area of the figure shown below in square units?**

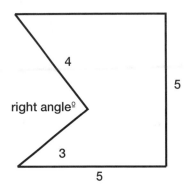

A   12

B   18

C   19

D   20

64. **A rectangular duck pond 43 feet by 47 feet is on a square lot 100 feet by 100 feet. The rest of the lot is a flower garden. Approximately how many square feet is the flower garden?**

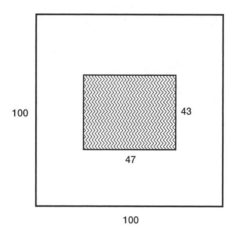

A   1,400

B   4,000

C   7,500

D   8,000

65. **A car is traveling at the rate of 40 miles per hour. How many minutes will it take to travel 220 miles?**

A   55

B   120

C   330

D   480

66. **What is the volume of the box shown below?**

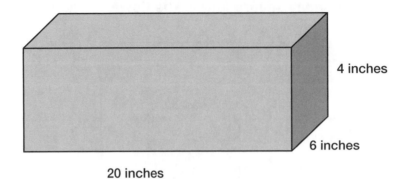

4 inches

6 inches

20 inches

A   480

B   720

C   800

D   880

67. **Approximately how many square centimeters is the area of the circle below?**

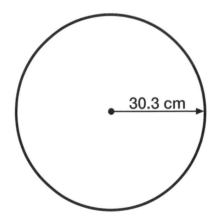

30.3 cm

A $3 \times 3 \times 3 = 27$

B $2 \times 3 \times 30 = 180$

C $3 \times 3 \times 30 = 270$

D $3 \times 30 \times 30 = 2,700$

68. **The table below shows the flight times from San Diego, California, to Memphis, Tennessee. Which flight takes the shortest amount of time?**

Leave San Diego time	Arrive Memphis time
9:00 a.m.	3:20 p.m.
11:00 a.m.	5:35 p.m.
4:30 p.m.	10:35 p.m.
8:45 p.m.	2:55 a.m.

   A The flight leaving at 9:00 a.m.

   B The flight leaving at 11:00 a.m.

   C The flight leaving at 4:30 p.m.

   D The flight leaving at 8:45 p.m.

69. **Solve $2(7x - 3) + 4(x - 2) = 22$ for x.**

   A 2

   B 4

   C 6

   D 8

70. **What are the coordinates of the y-intercept of the line $3x - 5y = 15$?**

   A (0, –5)

   B (0, –3)

   C (3, 0)

   D (5, 0)

71. Which of the following statements describes two lines that have the same slope but different *y*-intercepts?

    A   parallel

    B   intersecting

    C   perpendicular

    D   parabolic

72. Assume that *x* is an integer. Solve |*x* + 5| = 7 for *x*.

    A   {–2, 2}

    B   {–12, 12}

    C   {–2, 12}

    D   {–12, 2}

73. Which of the following points lies on the line expressed by the equation 2*x* + 3*y* = 12 ?

    A   (1, 4)

    B   (2, 3)

    C   (3, 2)

    D   (6, 1)

74. The length of the rectangle below is 2 units longer than the width. Which expression represents the area of the rectangle?

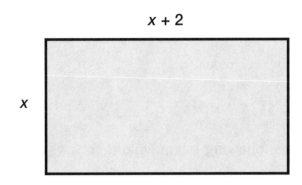

$x + 2$

x

A $\quad x^2 + 2$

B $\quad x^2 + 2x$

C $\quad x^2 + 2x + 2$

D $\quad x^2 + 4x + 8$

75. Which of the following is equivalent to the equation $\dfrac{6}{x+4} = \dfrac{10}{x}$?

A $\quad 6 = x(x + 4)$

B $\quad 6x = 10(x + 4)$

C $\quad 10x = 6(x + 4)$

D $\quad 10 = 6(x + 4)$

76. Assuming x is an integer, which of the following is a solution set for $4|x| = 24$?

A $\quad \{6\}$

B $\quad \{0, -6\}$

C $\quad \{0, 6\}$

D $\quad \{-6, 6\}$

77. Which is the best estimate of 21 × 483?

    A   100

    B   1,000

    C   10,000

    D   100,000

78. Which of the following is equivalent to $2x + 3 < 4(x - 1)$?

    A $2x + 3 < 4x - 1$

    B $2x + 3 < 4x - 2$

    C $2x + 3 < 4x - 4$

    D $2x + 3 < 4x - 5$

79. Which of the following is an equation of a line parallel to the line $y = 2x - 9$?

    A $y = \dfrac{1}{2}x + 9$

    B $y = -2x + 9$

    C $y = 2x + 7$

    D $y = -\dfrac{1}{2}x + 7$

80. **What is the solution to the system of equations shown below?**

$$\begin{cases} y = 2x - 3 \\ y = 3x \end{cases}$$

A   (4, –5)

B   (3, 0)

C   (–3, –9)

D   (6, 2)

Answer Key

1.	(A)	28.	(B)	55.	(C)
2.	(D)	29.	(C)	56.	(A)
3.	(B)	30.	(B)	57.	(D)
4.	(D)	31.	(A)	58.	(D)
5.	(C)	32.	(C)	59.	(A)
6.	(B)	33.	(A)	60.	(B)
7.	(A)	34.	(D)	61.	(C)
8.	(C)	35.	(C)	62.	(B)
9.	(B)	36.	(D)	63.	(C)
10.	(A)	37.	(C)	64.	(D)
11.	(D)	38.	(B)	65.	(C)
12.	(D)	39.	(C)	66.	(A)
13.	(D)	40.	(D)	67.	(D)
14.	(A)	41.	(B)	68.	(C)
15.	(C)	42.	(A)	69.	(A)
16.	(B)	43.	(B)	70.	(B)
17.	(C)	44.	(C)	71.	(A)
18.	(C)	45.	(B)	72.	(D)
19.	(C)	46.	(B)	73.	(C)
20.	(B)	47.	(B)	74.	(B)
21.	(B)	48.	(D)	75.	(B)
22.	(A)	49.	(D)	76.	(D)
23.	(D)	50.	(C)	77.	(C)
24.	(B)	51.	(B)	78.	(C)
25.	(B)	52.	(A)	79.	(C)
26.	(D)	53.	(A)	80.	(C)
27.	(C)	54.	(C)		

Detailed Explanations of Answers

PRACTICE TEST 1

1. **A**

$$\frac{3}{8} + \frac{4}{7} = \frac{7 \times 3}{7 \times 8} + \frac{8 \times 4}{8 \times 7} = \frac{21}{56} + \frac{32}{56} = \frac{53}{56}$$

2. **D**

$2.4 \times 10^3 = 2,400$

Since the exponent on the 10 is 3, move the decimal point 3 places to the right. The answer is 2,400.

3. **B**

$(-9) + (5) = -4$, which is a negative number.

4. **D**

$$\frac{15x^2y^4}{3xy^2} = 5x^{2-1}y^{4-2} = 5xy^2$$

5. **C**

First, find the amount saved. $15.00 – $12.00 = $3.00. Then, divide the amount saved by the original price.

$$15\overline{)3.00}$$
$$\underline{.20}$$
$$\underline{3.00}$$
$$0$$

Lastly, convert this decimal of 0.20 into a percentage by moving the decimal point 2 places to the right. The final answer is 20%.

6. **B**

Round 90 to 100 and round 190 to 200. Then, divide 100 by 200 which equals 1/2.

1/2 in percentage is 50%.

7. **A**

When multiplying terms with a common base, you add exponents.

$5^3 \times 5^7 = 5^{3+7} = 5^{10}$

8. **C**

First, multiply $32.00 times 20%. 20% in decimal form is 0.2.

$32.00 x 0.2 = $6.40

Then, subtract the saving from the regular price in order to find the sale price.

$32.00 – $6.40 = $25.60

9. **B**

First, find the probability of each outcome. Since a die has 6 sides, the probability of each outcome is 1/6. This question asks you to find the probability of rolling a 2 or a 3. Add the probabilities of each outcome.

1/6 + 1/6 = 2/6

2/6 in lowest terms is 1/3.

10. **A**

First, multiply 10 times 0 which equals 0. Then, multiply 10 times 1 which equals 10. Therefore, the number must be between 0 and 10.

11. **D**

There are a number of fractions that could represent 80%. Therefore, convert each fraction into a decimal and find out which fraction equals 0.8, because 0.8 is the decimal form of 80%. The answer is 4/5 because 4/5 = 0.8; (A) 1/4 = 0.25 or 25%, (B) 1/3 = $0.\overline{3}$ or about 33%, and (C) 3/8 = 0.375 or 37.5%.

12. **D**

Convert the words "five more than three times a number" into an expression. The term "five more" means to add five, and the term "three times a number" means multiply by three. Therefore, the expression $3x + 5$ is correct.

13. **D**

First, multiply the regular price by the percent off. In decimal form 15% is 0.15.

$60 × 0.15 = $9

Then, subtract the savings from the regular price.

$60 − $9 = $51

14. **A**

First, find the lowest common denominator for the numbers 6 and 7. The lowest common denominator is 42, because both 6 and 7 divide evenly into 42. Then, put 42 into prime factored form. A prime number is a number that can only be divided by one and itself. A factor divides evenly into a number.

2 × 3 × 7 = 42

Therefore, 2 × 3 × 7 is the final answer.

15. **C**

This question is really asking you to find the square root of 225 and then the square root of 400. Remember, squaring a number and taking the square root of a number are opposite operations.

The square root of 225 is 15 because 15 × 15 = 225. The square root of 400 is 20 because 20 × 20 = 400. Therefore, the final answer is between 15 and 20.

16. **B**

The absolute value of a number is just the positive form of that number. The absolute value of −7 is simply 7.

17. **C**

First, find 10% of $16.00. $16.00 × 0.1 = $1.60

Then, add 1/2 of $1.60, which is $0.80, to $1.60.

$1.60 + $.80 = $2.40

18. **C**

This question is really asking, "Which of the following answers can be divided evenly by the numbers 2, 5, and 8?" The answer is the number 40.

19. **C**

Round 216 to 200 and round 192 to 200. Then multiply.

200 × 200 = 40,000

20. **B**

In order to find the probability of a single outcome, you need to first list all possible outcomes from the experiment. If you flip a coin 2 times, there are four possible outcomes: {HH, HT, TH, TT}. Each outcome has a 1/4 chance of occurring. 1/4 in percentage terms is 25%. Therefore, the probability of rolling 2 heads in two flips of a fair coin is 25%.

21. **B**

In order to find Mary's mean score, add her scores for each of the four tests, and then divide by four.

9 + 8 + 10 + 5 = 32

32/4 = 8

22. Ⓐ

Tuesday has the greatest increase in temperature over that of the previous day.

The high temperature for Tuesday was 65, while for Monday, it was 50. The difference is a 15 degree increase. On Wednesday (B), the temperature *decreased* 10 degrees. On Thursday (C), the temperature increased 10 degrees, and on Friday (D), the temperature increased only 5 degrees.

23. Ⓓ

If there is a 35% chance of rain, then there is a 65% chance that it *does not* rain. The probability that it *does not* rain is equal to 100% minus the probability that it does rain.

100% – 35% = 65%

24. Ⓑ

Each flip of a coin is an independent event. Therefore, the probability that the coin lands heads is 1/2, no matter how many times it has just landed tails. The coin does not remember.

25. Ⓑ

The mode is the most frequently occurring score. Because the number 3 occurs more often than any other number in the set, it is the mode score.

26. Ⓓ

The number of complaints is not as important as the average number of complaints. This is because an average takes into consideration how long a company has been in business. SPEEDY delivery company has 100/25 or an average of four complaints per month.

However, ON TIME delivery company has 10/2 or an average of five complaints per month. Therefore, on average, ON TIME delivery company has more complaints per month. It is misleading for a company to say that they have less complaints than another company when they have not been in business as long.

27. **C**

Since there are four cards, each card has a 0.25 probability of being selected. This is because 1/4 = 0.25. Thus, the probability of selecting a heart is 0.25.

The probability of *not* selecting a heart is 1.0 − 0.25 = 0.75.

28. **B**

The warmest day of the week is Thursday. Tuesday is the second warmest while Wednesday is the third warmest. Starting from the point on the graph that marks Wednesday, look left at the temperature axis that shows 55 degrees.

29. **C**

The amount of rainfall is determined by looking at the length of the bars. First, find the shortest bar which is July, and the second shortest which is August. The third shortest is March. Next, looking left from March to the rainfall axis, you can see that March had 5 inches of rain.

30. **B**

In order to find the median, you must first rank order the scores like this:

0, 2, 3, 5, 6, 7, 12.

The median value is the score in the middle. The median is 5.

31. **A**

   Draw a line through the set of data points. Notice that low values of temperature go with high sales, and that high-temperature values go with low sales. Next, evaluate the truth of each possible answer. The graph shows that as temperature decreases, sales of jackets increase.

32. **C**

   The amount of rainfall is determined by the length of the bars used to make the graph. First, find the longest bar, which is October, then the second longest, which is November, then the third longest, which is December. Finally, the fourth-longest bar is May. May has the fourth-highest average monthly rainfall.

33. **A**

   Divide a number by 2 means $x/2$. Add 3 to the result means plus 3. The answer is 10 means equals 10. The final answer is $x/2 + 3 = 10$.

34. **D**

   The general equation for a line is $y = mx + b$ where m is the slope and b is the y-intercept. The slope is equal to rise over run, so the slope of the line in the graph is equal to 1/1 or 1. The y-intercept is the point at which the line crosses the y-axis, so the y-intercept of the line is equal to 2. Therefore, the equation of the line is $y = x + 2$.

35. **C**

   Draw a line through the set of data points. Notice that low grade levels go with low hours of reading, and that high grade levels go with high hours of reading. Next, evaluate the truth of each possible answer. The graph shows that as the grade level goes up, the number of reading hours goes up.

36. **D**

The graph of the function *y* equals *x* squared is called a parabola.

(A) This is a graph of *y* equals negative *x* to the third power.

(B) This is a graph of *y* equals *x*.

(C) This is a graph of *y* equals negative *x*.

37. **C**

$(3xy^2)(7x^2y^3) = 21x^{1+2}y^{2+3} = 21x^3y^5$

38. **B**

Solve for *x* means to get *x* by itself.

$3x + 5 < 20$

$3x < 20 - 5$

$3x < 15$

$\dfrac{3x}{3} < \dfrac{15}{3}$

$x < 5$

39. **C**

The variable on the *x*-axis is "Balance in $1,000." The variable on the *y*-axis is "Interest rate in %." One line represents Bank A and one line represents Bank B. Notice that the two lines cross each other at $3,000. For balances of more than $3,000, Bank A pays more interest than Bank B.

40. **D**

Let g equal the number of girls, and let b equal the number of boys. The number of boys as equal to four times the number of girls is expressed by $4 \times g = b$.

41. **B**

The variable on the x-axis is number of music CDs. The variable on the y-axis is total cost. The price of each CD can be read from finding one CD on the x-axis, going up until you hit the line, then reading the cost on the y-axis. One CD costs $20.

42. **A**

This question is asking you to substitute 2 for x and 5 for y. Then, perform the indicated operations in the equation to come up with a single number.

$$\frac{xy + 4}{2} - 3 = \frac{(2)(5) + 4}{2} - 3$$

$$= \frac{10 + 4}{2} - 3$$

$$= \frac{14}{2} - 3$$

$$= 7 - 3$$

$$= 4$$

43. **B**

$$(5x^3y^2z)(9xy^2z) = 45x^{3+1}y^{2+2}z^{1+1} = 45x^4y^4z^2$$

44. **C**

Solve for *x* means to get *x* by itself.

$4x + 4 = 7$

$4x = 7 - 4$

$4x = 3$

$\dfrac{4x}{4} = \dfrac{3}{4}$

$x = \dfrac{3}{4}$

45. **B**

Slope is equal to rise over run. In the figure, you can see that the rise is 3 and the run is 2. Therefore, the slope is 3 over 2 or 3/2.

46. **B**

Divide 20 by 2.5 in order to find out how many minutes it will take to fill the gas tank. 20 divided by 2.5 equals 8.

47. **B**

Draw a line through the points given but also extend this line downward. Next, find the year 1995 on the *x*-axis and then go up until you hit the line that you have drawn. Then, read the number of oranges produced on the *y*-axis. The answer is 10,000.

48. **D**

Solve for *x* means to get *x* by itself.

$$\frac{x}{3} - 2 = 8$$

$$\frac{x}{3} = 8 + 2$$

$$\frac{x}{3} = 10$$

$$\frac{(3)x}{3} = 10(3)$$

$$x = 30$$

49. D

In order to calculate the average number of miles per gallon, you need to know two different variables—miles and gallons. This question gives you the number of gallons, but *not* the number of miles traveled. The fact that the truck made 100 different deliveries is irrelevant information.

50. C

Average speed is expressed in terms of "miles per hour." *Per* means *divide,* so divide miles by hours. Thus, 376 divided by 8 equals 47.

51. B

Multiply the number of centimeters in one inch by ten.

2.54 × 10 = 25.4

This is approximately equal to 25.

52. **A**

In order to answer this question, you need to use the Pythagorean theorem. The Pythagorean theorem tells you about the relationships between the length of the sides of a right triangle. The Pythagorean theorem is $a^2 + b^2 = c^2$, where a and b are the sides, and c is the hypotenuse. The hypotenuse is the side opposite the right angle. The present question is really asking you to find c.

$$a^2 + b^2 = c^2$$

$$4^2 + 3^2 = c^2$$

$$16 + 9 = c^2$$

$$25 = c^2$$

$$\sqrt{25} = \sqrt{c^2}$$

$$c = 5$$

53. **A**

Divide the number of square feet by nine.

$$135/9 = 15$$

There are 15 square yards in 135 square feet.

54. **C**

See the shaded region as being made up of four separate triangles. Calculate the area of one triangle using the formula *one-half its base times its height*, or in formula form: $1/2bh$. In the present problem, the base is 3 and the height is 3.

$$\frac{1}{2}(3)(3) = \frac{1}{2}(9) = 4.5$$

This is the area of one triangle. Since there are four triangles in the shaded region, multiply this area times four. Thus, $4.5 \times 4 = 18$. The final answer is 18 square inches.

55. **C**

This question is asking you to find the circumference of a circle using this formula: circumference equals pi times the diameter. However, in this question you are given the length of the radius which is 5 inches. The diameter is equal to the radius times two, so the diameter is equal to 2(5) = 10 inches. Now, use the formula $C = \pi d$; $\pi = 3.14$.

$$C = 3.14(10) = 31.4 \approx 31$$

The circumference of the circle is approximately equal to 31 inches.

56. **A**

Find the *y*-axis. Find the side of the figure closest to the *y*-axis and measure the distance that this side is from the *y*-axis. A reflection of the figure will put this side the same distance from the *y*-axis, but on the other side.

Also, notice the point labeled C. A reflection of this point across the *y*-axis will also be the same distance from the *y*-axis, but on the other side.

57. **D**

Use the formula 1/2*bh*.

$$\frac{1}{2}(16)(6) = \frac{1}{2}(96) = 48$$

The triangle has an area of 48 square inches. Note: The length of the side that equals 10 inches is irrelevant.

58. **D**

Multiply the number of cubic centimeters in one cubic inch by two.

2 × 16.38 = 32.76

There are approximately 32.76 cubic centimeters in two cubic inches.

59. **A**

First, make use of the fact that the sum of the angles of any triangle is 180 degrees. The missing angle in the second triangle can be found by adding the two angles and then subtracting from 180.

80 + 30 = 110

180 − 110 = 70

The missing angle equals 70 degrees. Now compare the two triangles. You can see that both triangles have an angle 70 degrees, a side 8 inches, and an angle 30 degrees. Therefore, by the Angle-Side-Angle postulate, the two triangles are congruent.

60. **B**

The formula for the area of a triangle is $\frac{1}{2}bh$ where b equals base, and h equals height. The area of triangle A equals $\frac{1}{2}(5)(2) = \frac{1}{2}(10) = 5$. The area of triangle B equals $\frac{1}{2}(10)(4) = \frac{1}{2}(40) = 20$. Lastly, divide the area of triangle A by the area of triangle B, and put this fraction into lowest terms.

$$\frac{5}{20} = \frac{1}{4}$$

61. **C**

Plot the points given on an *x, y* graph. Then, connect the nearest points. The figure created is called a parallelogram. A parallelogram is a figure with four sides, having the opposite sides parallel and equal.

62. **B**

In the scaled drawing, length is equal to 3¹/₄ inches or, in decimal form, 3.25 inches. The scale is "1 inch equals 24 feet." In order to find the length in feet, multiply the number of inches times 24.

$3.25 \times 24 = 78$

63. **C**

See this figure as a square with a triangle removed. Calculate the area of the triangle. Area equals $\frac{1}{2}(3)(4) = \frac{1}{2}(12) = 6$. Then, calculate the area of the square. Area equals $5 \times 5 = 25$. Lastly, in order to find the area of the actual figure, subtract the area of the triangle from the area of the square.

$25 - 6 = 19$

64. **D**

First, calculate the area of the duck pond. Round 47 to 50, and round 43 to 40. Next, multiply: $50 \times 40 = 2,000$. The area of the duck pond is 2,000 square feet. Now, calculate the area of the lot: $100 \times 100 = 10,000$. Lastly, in order to find the approximate area of the flower garden, subtract the area of the duck pond from the area of the lot.

$10,000 - 2,000 = 8,000$

The flower garden is approximately 8,000 square feet.

65. **C**

Use the formula: distance equals rate times time. In this question, you are given the rate, and you are given the distance. In order to solve for time, divide distance by rate thusly: 220 divided by 40 equals 5.5 hours. However, this question is asking for time in minutes. In order to convert hours into minutes, multiply by 60.

5.5 × 60 = 330

66. **A**

Calculate volume by multiplying height times width times length.

4 × 6 × 20 = 480

67. **D**

The formula given for the area of a circle is pi times r squared. Pi is approximately equal to 3.14 or more approximately 3, while *r* is equal to the radius of the circle. In this question, *r* is equal to 30.3 or approximately 30. The equation for area is pi times *r squared*. *r* squared equals *r* times *r*. Therefore, the approximate area of the circle is 3 × 30 × 30 = 2,700.

68. **C**

Determine the length of the trips in parts. For the first trip (A), there are 3 hours between 9:00 a.m. and 12:00 p.m., and there are 3 hours and 20 minutes between 12:00 p.m. and 3:20 p.m. So, the entire trip takes 6 hours and 20 minutes. Similarly, the second trip (B) takes 6 hours 35 minutes, the third trip (C) takes 6 hours and 5 minutes, and the last trip (D) takes 6 hours and 10 minutes. So, the third trip (C) is the shortest.

69. **A**

Solve for *x* means to get *x* by itself.

$$2(7x - 3) + 4(x - 2) = 22$$

$$14x - 6 + 4x - 8 = 22$$

$$18x - 14 = 22$$

$$18x = 22 + 14$$

$$18x = 36$$

$$\frac{18x}{18} = \frac{36}{18}$$

$$x = 2$$

70. **B**

In order to find the coordinates of the *y*-intercept of a line, let *x* equal 0 and solve for *y*.

$$3x - 5y = 15$$

$$3(0) - 5y = 15$$

$$-5y = 15$$

$$\frac{-5y}{-5} = \frac{15}{-5}$$

$$y = -3$$

Therefore, the coordinates of the *y*-intercept are (0, –3).

71. **A**

Parallel lines have the same slope but different *y*-intercepts. Intersecting lines (B) have different slopes. Perpendicular lines (C) cross each other at a 90-degree angle. Parabolic (D) describes a curved function, not a line.

72. **D**

This equation has an absolute value sign in it. An absolute value means the positive value of a number. The equation given is $|x + 5| = 7$. This is read, "the absolute value of $x + 5$ equals 7." There are two possible answers to this equation. Either,

$x + 5 = -7$	or	$x + 5 = 7$
$x = -7 - 5$	or	$x = 7 - 5$
$x = -12$	or	$x = 2$

The final answer is $\{-12, 2\}$.

73. **C**

In order to find which point lies on the line expressed by an equation, plug each (x, y) point into the equation, one at a time, until you find a point that makes the equation true. The multiple choices are: (1, 4) (2, 3) (3, 2) (6, 1)

$2x + 3y = 12$	is the equation given.
$2(1) + 3(4) = 14$	This does not equal 12.
$2(2) + 3(3) = 13$	This does not equal 12.
$2(3) + 3(2) = 12$	*This does equal 12.* This point (3, 2) falls on the line $2x + 3y = 12$
$2(6) + 3(1) = 15$	This does not equal 12.

The final answer is the point (3, 2).

74. **B**

In order to find the area of a rectangle, multiply width times length. The width is x while the length is $x + 2$.

$$x(x + 2) = x^2 + 2x$$

75. **B**

Answering this question involves getting rid of the denominators by cross multiplying.

$$\frac{6}{x+4} = \frac{10}{x}$$

$$\frac{6}{x+4} \diagdown\!\!\!\!\diagup \frac{10}{x}$$

$$6x = 10(x + 4)$$

76. **D**

The equation $4|x| = 24$ has an absolute value sign in it. The absolute value of a number is always positive. There are two solutions to this equation. The two solutions are −6 and 6.

$4|x| = 24$

$4|{-}6| = 24$

$4|6| = 24$

The final answer is {−6, 6}

77. **C**

First, round the number 483 to 500. Second, round the number 21 to 20. Then multiply: 500 times 20 equals 10,000.

78. **C**

Solving this problem requires distributing the number in front of the parentheses across both terms inside of the parentheses.

$4(x − 1) = 4x − 4$

Therefore, $2x + 3 < 4(x − 1)$ is equivalent to $2x + 3 < 4x − 4$.

79. **C**

The general form for the equation of a line is $y = mx + b$ where m is the slope and b is the y-intercept. *Parallel lines have the same slope.* Inspect each of the multiple choices until you find a line that has the same slope. In the equation $y = 2x - 9$, the slope is 2. Therefore, the line $y = 2x + 7$ is parallel to it.

80. **C**

This question is really asking, "Which of the following points will make both equations true?" In order to answer this question, try each (x, y) point, one at a time, until you find a point that makes *both* equations true. The multiple choices are: (4, –5) (3, 0) (–3, –9) (6, 2)

$y = 2x - 3$

$y = 3x$

| $-5 = 2(4) - 3$ | $-5 = 5$ | false |
| $-5 = 3(4)$ | $-5 = 12$ | false |

| $0 = 2(3) - 3$ | $0 = 3$ | false |
| $0 = 3(3)$ | $0 = 9$ | false |

| $-9 = 2(-3) - 3$ | $-9 = -9$ | true |
| $-9 = 3(-3)$ | $-9 = -9$ | true |

The point (–3, –9) makes both equations true.

| $2 = 2(6) - 3$ | $2 = 9$ | false |
| $2 = 3(6)$ | $2 = 18$ | false |

The final answer is the point (–3, –9).

CAHSEE

Practice Test 2

Practice Test 2

1. $\dfrac{3}{5} + \dfrac{2}{25} =$

   A $\dfrac{6}{25}$

   B $\dfrac{17}{25}$

   C $\dfrac{7}{50}$

   D $\dfrac{12}{50}$

* Reprinted by permission of California High School Exit Exam (CAHSEE), California Department of Education, P.O. Box 271, Sacramento, CA 95812-0271.

2. **$7.9 \times 10^2 =$**

   A   7.900

   B   79

   C   790

   D   7,900

3. **Which of the following equals a negative number?**

   A $(-4) + (6)$

   B $(-6) + (4)$

   C $(4) + (6)$

   D $(4) + (-6) + (3)$

4. $\dfrac{24x^3y^5}{6x^2y} =$

   A $4xy^5$

   B $4x^6y^5$

   C $4x^5y^6$

   D $4xy^4$

5. **Music CDs are on sale. The original price was $20.00. The sale price is $15.00. What is the percent saving?**

   A   5%

   B   10%

   C   20%

   D   25%

6. In her softball games this year, Carla got a hit 7 times out of 20 times at bat. What percent of the time did Carla get a hit?

   A 25%

   B 35%

   C 45%

   D 55%

7. $3^2 \times 3^5 =$

   A 3^7

   B 3^{10}

   C 9^7

   D 9^{10}

8. Baseball caps regularly cost $16.00. They are on sale for 25% off. What is the sale price of the baseball caps?

   A $8

   B $10

   C $12

   D $14

9. A die has six sides. What is the probability of rolling a 4, a 5, or a 6 in one throw of a fair die?

   A $\dfrac{1}{6}$

   B $\dfrac{1}{3}$

C $\dfrac{1}{2}$

D $\dfrac{2}{3}$

10. One thousand is multiplied by a number between 0 and 1. The answer has to be between which two numbers?

A 0 and 100

B 0 and 1,000

C 0 and 100 but not 50

D 0 and 1,000 but not 500

11. Which fraction does 40% equal?

A $\dfrac{1}{4}$

B $\dfrac{2}{5}$

C $\dfrac{3}{4}$

D $\dfrac{4}{5}$

12. On a math quiz, Tony is asked to write down the mathematical expression for the words, "eight more than five times a number." Tony *incorrectly* answers 13x. Which expression should he have used?

A 8x

B 8(5x)

C $8x + 5$

D $5x + 8$

13. **A local department store is having a sale. All swim suits are 15% off. What is the sale price of a swim suit that is regularly $30?**

    A $24.00

    B $25.50

    C $26.00

    D $27.50

14. **Which of the following is the prime factored form of the lowest common denominator of $\dfrac{3}{8} + \dfrac{4}{7}$?**

    A 7×8

    B $2 \times 2 \times 7$

    C $2 \times 3 \times 7$

    D $2 \times 2 \times 2 \times 7$

15. **A whole number is squared and the result is between 400 and 625. The number must be between _____.**

    A 5 and 10

    B 10 and 15

    C 15 and 20

    D 20 and 25

16. The absolute value of −9 is equal to which of the following?

    A $-\dfrac{1}{9}$

    B   −9

    C $\dfrac{1}{9}$

    D   9

17. When eating at a restaurant, a common practice is to tip the waiter or waitress 15% of the price of the meal. An easy way to calculate the tip is to take 10% of the bill, plus 1/2 of that. Using this rule, if a restaurant bill comes to $24.00, how much should the tip be?

    A $2.40

    B $3.00

    C $3.60

    D $4.00

18. The winning number in a drawing is less than 50. It is a multiple of 2, 6, and 7. What is the number?

    A   30

    B   36

    C   42

    D   48

19. What is the best estimate of 311 × 489?

    A   150

B 1,500

C 15,000

D 150,000

20. **A fair coin is flipped three times. What is the probability of getting 3 heads?**

A $\dfrac{1}{8}$

B $\dfrac{1}{4}$

C $\dfrac{1}{2}$

D $\dfrac{3}{4}$

21. **The chart below shows the English test scores of three students.**

	Test 1	Test 2	Test 3	Test 4
Peter	10	7	5	4
Paul	3	6	9	10
Mary	9	8	10	5

What is Paul's mean score?

A 7

B 8

C 9

D 10

22. **The graph below represents the high temperature for five days of the week.**

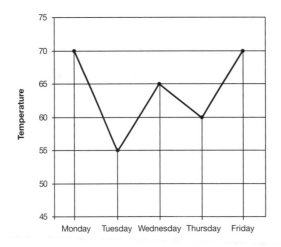

Which day has the smallest change in temperature over that of the previous day?

A   Tuesday

B   Wednesday

C   Thursday

D   Friday

23. **A weather person on the evening news says that there is a 20% chance that it rains tomorrow. What is the probability that it *does not* rain?**

A   10%

B   25%

C   50%

D   80%

24. Alex flips a coin 5 times, and each time it comes up heads. If he flips the coin one more time, what is the probability that it will come up heads?

    A $\dfrac{1}{5}$

    B $\dfrac{1}{2}$

    C $\dfrac{6}{10}$

    D $\dfrac{9}{10}$

25. What is the mode score for the following set of scores?

    { 4, 5, 9, 6, 5, 7, 4, 7, 5, 4, 3, 5 }

    A 3

    B 4

    C 5

    D 7

26. GREEN TAXI company uses the data in the table below to support their claim, "We have one-fifth the number of customer complaints that BLUE TAXI company has." Why is this claim misleading?

Taxi Company	Customer Complaints	Months in Business
BLUE TAXI	100	25
GREEN TAXI	20	4

A   On average, BLUE TAXI has more complaints.

B   The claim should say "one-fourth" the number of complaints.

C   The claim should say "one-sixth" the number of complaints.

D   On average, GREEN TAXI has more complaints *per month*.

27.   **Five cards are shown below; a heart, a diamond, a moon, a sun, and a lightning bolt. If you randomly select a single card, what is the probability that it is *not* a heart?**

A   0.75
B   0.80
C   0.85
D   0.90

28.   **Using the graph shown below, what is the temperature for the second-coldest day of the week?**

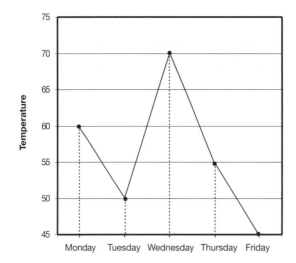

A 45

B 50

C 60

D 70

29. **The graph below shows the average monthly rainfall for the city of Pinewood. During the month that had the fourth-largest amount of rainfall, how many inches did it rain?**

**Average Monthly Rainfall for the
City of Pinewood**

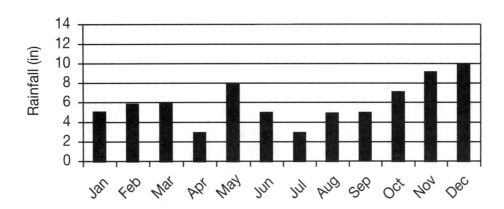

A 7

B 8

C 9

D 10

30. Cathy scores the following points in her high school basketball games: 8, 2, 5, 9, 0, 4, 7.

    What is her median number of points scored?

    A   2

    B   5

    C   7

    D   9

31. **The graph below shows the relationship between variable *x* and variable *y*. Which statement does this graph support?**

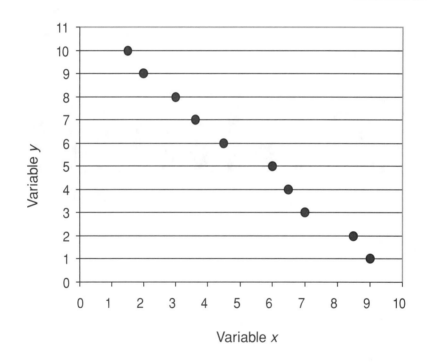

    A   As variable *x* increases, variable *y* decreases.

    B   As variable *x* increases, variable *y* increases.

    C   As variable *x* decreases, variable *y* decreases.

    D   Variable *x* and variable *y* are unrelated.

32. The graph below shows the average monthly rainfall for the city of Booneville. Which month has the third-lowest average monthly rainfall?

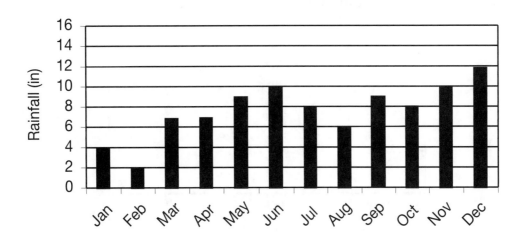

Average Monthly Rainfall for the City of Booneville

A January

B April

C August

D October

33. Divide a number by 3 and add 5 to the result. The answer is 9. Which of the following equations expresses these statements?

A $\dfrac{x}{3} + 5 = 9$

B $\dfrac{x}{8} = 9$

C $\quad 5 = \dfrac{x}{3} + 9$

D $\quad \dfrac{x + 5}{3} = 9$

34. **What is the equation of the line shown below?**

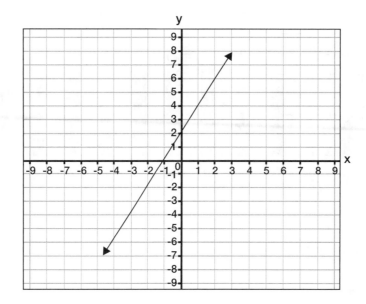

A $\quad y = 2x + 2$

B $\quad y = 2x - 2$

C $\quad y = \dfrac{1}{2}x - 2$

D $\quad y = \dfrac{1}{2}x + 2$

35. **The scatter plot below shows the relationship between temperature and air pollen count. Which statement describes this relationship?**

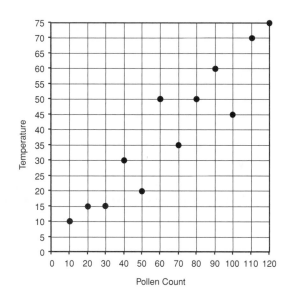

A   As temperature goes down, pollen count tends to go up.

B   As temperature goes up, pollen count tends to go down.

C   As temperature goes up, pollen count tends to go up.

D   Temperature and pollen count are unrelated.

36. **Which of the graphs below could be the graph of** *y* = *x* **?**

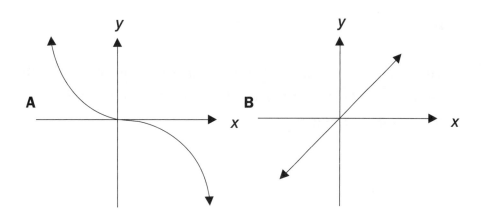

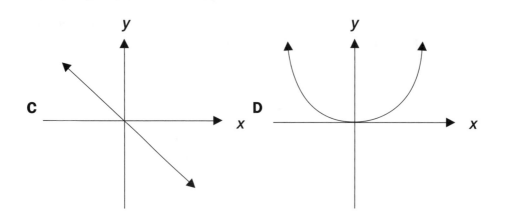

37. Simplify the following expression: $(4xy^2)(8x^3y^4)$

    A $32x^2y^2$

    B $32x^3y^6$

    C $32x^4y^6$

    D $32x^3y^8$

38. Given $2x - 6 > 10$, solve for x.

    A $x > 2$

    B $x > 4$

    C $x > 6$

    D $x > 8$

39. The graph below shows the interest rate paid by two different banks on a savings account. The interest rate depends upon the amount of the balance.

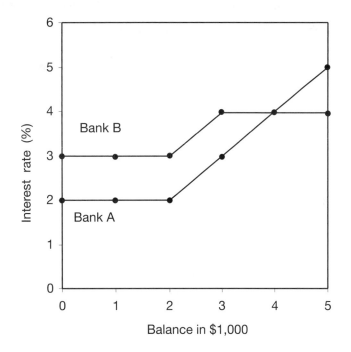

Bank A pays less interest than Bank B for balances of _____.

A $4,000 only

B   less than $4,000

C   more than $4,000

D   all amounts

40. In a certain class, the number of boys, *b,* is equal to three times the number of girls, *g*. Which of the following equations expresses this sentence?

A $3 \cdot b = g$

B $3 \cdot b = g \cdot b$

C $g \cdot b = 3$

D $3 \cdot g = b$

41. The graph below shows the relationship between the number of CDs purchased and the total cost. What is the price of each CD?

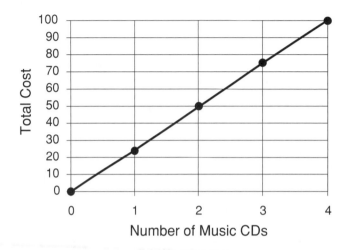

A $20.00

B $25.00

C $27.50

D $30.00

42. If $x = 6$ and $y = 7$, then $\dfrac{xy - 4}{2} - 5 =$

A 12

B 14

C 16

D 18

43. Simplify the following: $(9xy^2z)(9xy^3z^4)$

A $81xy^5z^4$

B $81x^2y^5z^5$

C $81x^2y^6z^4$

D $81xy^3z^4$

44. **Given $5x + 2 = 6$, solve for x.**

A $\dfrac{1}{4}$

B $\dfrac{1}{2}$

C $\dfrac{2}{3}$

D $\dfrac{4}{5}$

45. **What is the slope of the line below?**

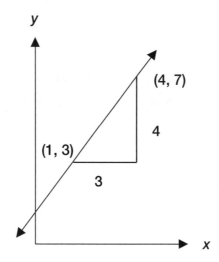

A $-\dfrac{3}{4}$

B $\dfrac{4}{3}$

C $\dfrac{3}{4}$

D $-\dfrac{4}{3}$

46. A gasoline pump pumps gas at the rate of 3.2 gallons a minute. At this rate, how many minutes will it take to fill a car with a gas tank that holds 16 gallons?

A 5

B 8

C 10

D 12

47. The graph below shows the number of apples produced by a grower in Washington for the years 1995, 1997, and 1999.

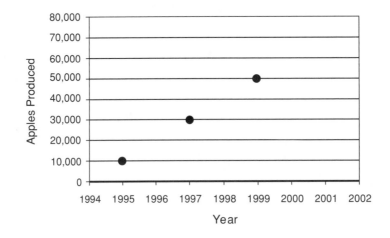

From this graph, which of the following was the most probable number of apples produced by this grower in 2001?

A 50,000

B 60,000

C 70,000

D 80,000

48. Given $\dfrac{x}{7} - 2 = 5$, solve for x.

A 49

B 56

C 63

D 70

49. What other information is needed in order to solve this problem?

A delivery truck made 100 different deliveries in one week and traveled 250 miles. What was the average number of miles per gallon?

A the average number of deliveries made each day

B the cost of gasoline per gallon

C the average speed per hour

D the number of gallons used

50. A train travels 120 miles from Los Angeles to San Diego. The trip takes $2\dfrac{1}{2}$ hours. What is the average speed of the train in miles per hour (mph)?

A   35 mph

B   38 mph

C   48 mph

D   60 mph

51. **There are approximately 2.54 centimeters in one inch. Approximately how many centimeters are there in 100 inches?**

A   2.5

B   25

C   250

D   2500

52. **What is the value of *x* in the triangle shown below?**

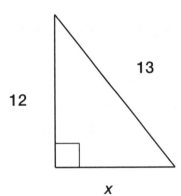

A   3

B   4

C   5

D   6

53. There are 9 square feet in one square yard. How many square yards are there in 198 square feet?

   A   20

   B   22

   C   28

   D   32

54. What is the area of the *unshaded* region in the figure shown below?

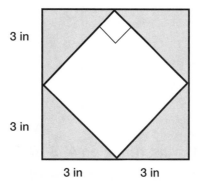

   A   4.5 in²

   B   9 in²

   C   18 in²

   D   32 in²

55. What is the approximate circumference of the circle shown below?

   ($\pi \approx 3.14$)

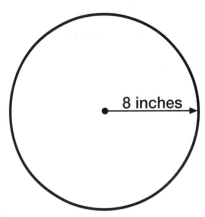

8 inches

A   25 inches

B   50 inches

C   75 inches

D   100 inches

56. **Which of the following triangles A′ B′ C′ is the image of triangle ABC that results from reflecting the triangle ABC across the *x*-axis?**

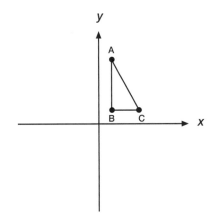

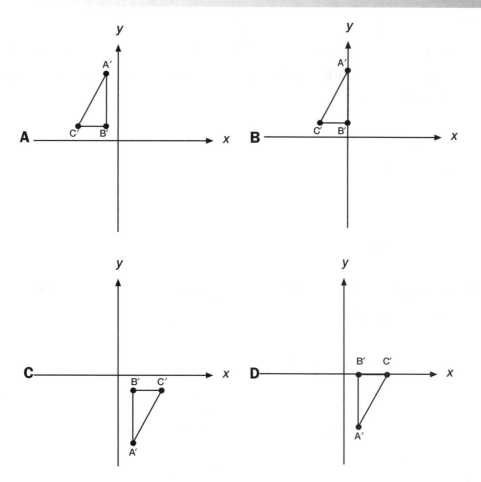

57. What is the area of the triangle shown below?

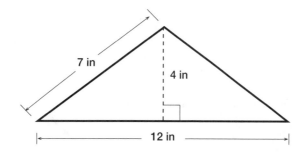

A   24 square inches

B   32 square inches

C   40 square inches

D   48 square inches

58. Approximately how many cubic centimeters are there in 4 cubic inches? (One cubic inch is approximately equal to 16.38 cubic centimeters.)

   A   32.76

   B   49.14

   C   65.52

   D   81.90

59. In the triangle shown below, what is the value of the missing angle in degrees?

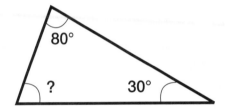

   A   36

   B   40

   C   60

   D   70

60. Two triangles are shown below.

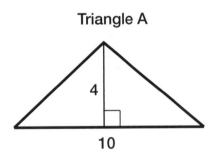

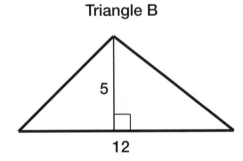

   What is $\dfrac{\text{the area of Triangle A}}{\text{the area of Triangle B}}$?

A $\dfrac{1}{8}$

B $\dfrac{1}{4}$

C $\dfrac{2}{3}$

D $\dfrac{4}{5}$

61. **The points (1, 1), (1, 4), (4, 1), (4, 4) are the vertices of a polygon. What type of polygon is formed by these points?**

   A Triangle

   B Square

   C Parallelogram

   D Trapezoid

62. **The scaled drawing of a volleyball court shown below is drawn using the scale 1 centimeter is equal to 2 meters.**

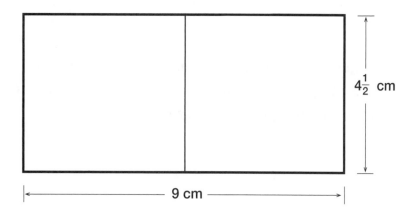

What is the area of the volleyball court in square meters?

A   40.5

B   81

C   162

D   205

63. **What is the area of the figure shown below in square units?**

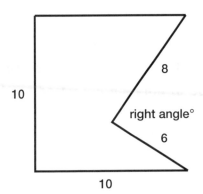

A   48

B   72

C   76

D   80

64. **A rectangular flower garden 52 feet by 57 feet is on a rectangular lot 104 feet by 96 feet. The rest of the lot is a lawn. Approximately how many square feet is the lawn?**

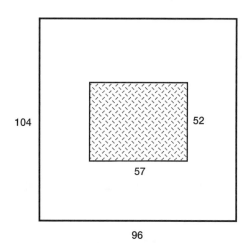

A 1,400

B 4,000

C 7,000

D 8,000

65. **A car is traveling at the rate of 45 miles per hour. How many minutes will it take to travel 270 miles?**

A 55

B 120

C 360

D 480

66. **What is the volume of the box shown below in cubic inches?**

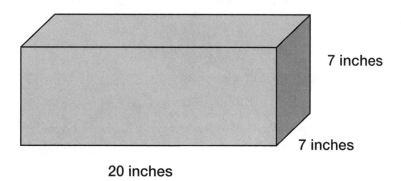

A   480

B   720

C   800

D   980

67. Approximately how many square centimeters is the area of the circle below?

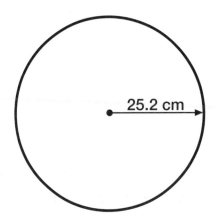

25.2 cm

A   3 × 3 × 3 = 27

B   2 × 3 × 25 = 150

C   3 × 3 × 25 = 225

D   3 × 25 × 25 = 1,875

68. The table below shows the flight times from Los Angeles, California, to Dallas, Texas. Which flight takes the shortest amount of time?

Leave Los Angeles time	Arrive Dallas time
9:00 a.m.	1:20 p.m.
11:00 a.m.	3:35 p.m.
4:30 p.m.	8:55 p.m.
8:45 p.m.	1:15 a.m.

A   The flight leaving at 9:00 a.m.

B   The flight leaving at 11:00 a.m.

C   The flight leaving at 4:30 p.m.

D   The flight leaving at 8:45 p.m.

69. **Solve $5(4x - 2) + 3(x + 1) = 39$ for x.**

A   2

B   4

C   6

D   8

70. **What are the coordinates of the *y*-intercept of the line $8x - 10y = 40$?**

A   (0, −5)

B   (0, −4)

C   (4, 0)

D   (5, 0)

71. **Two lines are parallel when they have the same _____ .**

A   *x*-intercept

B   *y*-intercept

C   slope

D   equation

72. **Assume that *x* is an integer. Solve |*x* + 8| = 12 for *x*.**

    A   {–4, 4}

    B   {–4, 20}

    C   {–20, 20}

    D   {–20, 4}

73. **Which of the following points lies on the line expressed by the equation 9*x* + 4*y* = 55 ?**

    A   (1, 4)

    B   (7, 3)

    C   (3, 2)

    D   (3, 7)

74. **The length of the rectangle below is 3 units longer than the width.**

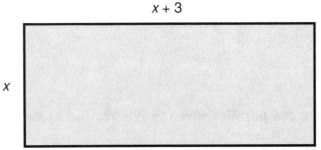

$x + 3$

x

    Which expression represents the area of the rectangle?

    A $x^2 + 3$

    B $x^2 + 3x$

    C $x^2 + 3x + 3$

    D $x^2 + 6x + 9$

75. Which of the following is equivalent to the equation shown below?

$$\frac{5}{x-1} = \frac{8}{x}$$

   A $5x = 8(x - 1)$

   B $5 = 8(x - 1)$

   C $8x = 5(x - 1)$

   D $8 = 5(x - 1)$

76. Assuming x is an integer, which of the following is a solution set for $8|x| = 32$?

   A $\{4\}$

   B $\{0, -4\}$

   C $\{0, 4\}$

   D $\{-4, 4\}$

77. Which is the best estimate of 179×222?

   A   4,000

   B   40,000

   C   400,000

   D   4,000,000

78. Which of the following is equivalent to $3x - 2 > 5(x + 3)$?

   A $3x - 2 > 5x + 3$

   B $3x - 2 > 5x + 5$

C $3x - 2 > 5x + 8$

D $3x - 2 > 5x + 15$

79. **Which of the following is an equation of a line parallel to the line**
    $y = 3x - 5$ **?**

    A $y = \dfrac{1}{3}x - 5$

    B $y = -3x + 5$

    C $y = 3x + 7$

    D $y = -\dfrac{1}{3}x + 5$

80. **What is the solution to the system of equations shown below?**

$$\begin{cases} y = 5x - 3 \\ y = 4x \end{cases}$$

    A $(2, 7)$

    B $(3, 12)$

    C $(4, 17)$

    D $(5, 22)$

Answer Key

1.	(B)	28.	(B)	55.	(B)
2.	(C)	29.	(A)	56.	(C)
3.	(B)	30.	(B)	57.	(A)
4.	(D)	31.	(A)	58.	(C)
5.	(D)	32.	(C)	59.	(D)
6.	(B)	33.	(A)	60.	(C)
7.	(A)	34.	(A)	61.	(B)
8.	(C)	35.	(C)	62.	(C)
9.	(C)	36.	(B)	63.	(C)
10.	(B)	37.	(C)	64.	(C)
11.	(B)	38.	(D)	65.	(C)
12.	(D)	39.	(B)	66.	(D)
13.	(B)	40.	(D)	67.	(D)
14.	(D)	41.	(B)	68.	(A)
15.	(D)	42.	(B)	69.	(A)
16.	(D)	43.	(B)	70.	(B)
17.	(C)	44.	(D)	71.	(C)
18.	(C)	45.	(B)	72.	(D)
19.	(D)	46.	(A)	73.	(D)
20.	(A)	47.	(C)	74.	(B)
21.	(A)	48.	(A)	75.	(A)
22.	(C)	49.	(D)	76.	(D)
23.	(D)	50.	(C)	77.	(B)
24.	(B)	51.	(C)	78.	(D)
25.	(C)	52.	(C)	79.	(C)
26.	(D)	53.	(B)	80.	(B)
27.	(B)	54.	(C)		

Detailed Explanations of Answers

PRACTICE TEST 2

1. B

$$\frac{3}{5} + \frac{2}{25} = \frac{5 \times 3}{5 \times 5} + \frac{2}{25} = \frac{15}{25} + \frac{2}{25} = \frac{17}{25}$$

2. C

Since the exponent on the 10 is 2, this means move the decimal point two places to the right. The answer is 790.

$7.9 \times 10^2 = 790$

3. B

$(-6) + (4) = -2$, which is a negative number.

4.   **D**

$$\frac{24x^3y^5}{6x^2y} = 4x^{3-2}y^{5-1} = 4xy^4$$

5.   **D**

First, find the amount saved, as follows: $20.00 – $15.00 = $5.00. Then, divide the amount saved by the original price.

```
        .25
   20)5.00
      4.00
      1.00
      1.00
      ────
         0
```

Lastly, convert this decimal of 0.25 into a percentage by moving the decimal point 2 places to the right. The final answer is 25%.

6.   **B**

Divide the number of hits by the number of at-bats.

7/20 = 0.35

Convert this decimal into a percentage. The final answer is 35%.

7.   **A**

When multiplying terms with a common base, you add exponents.

$3^2 \times 3^5 = 3^{2+5} = 3^7$

8.   **C**

First, multiply $16.00 times 25%. 25% in decimal form is 0.25.

$16.00 × 0.25 = $4.00

Then, subtract the saving from the regular price in order to find the sale price.

$16.00 – $4.00 = $12.00

9. **C**

First, find the probability of each outcome. Since a die has 6 sides, the probability of each outcome is 1/6. This question asks you to find the probability of rolling a 4, a 5, or a 6. Add the probabilities of each outcome.

1/6 + 1/6 + 1/6 = 3/6

3/6 in lowest terms is 1/2.

10. **B**

First, multiply 1,000 times 0; this equals 0. Then, multiply 1,000 times 1, this equals 1,000. Therefore, the number must be between 0 and 1,000.

11. **B**

There are a number of fractions that could represent 40%. Therefore, convert each fraction into a decimal and find out which fraction equals 0.4, because 0.4 is the decimal form of 40%.

The answer is 2/5 because 2/5 = 0.4; (A) 1/4 = 0.25 or 25%, (C) 3/4 = 0.75 or 75%, and (D) 4/5 = 0.8 or 80%.

12. **D**

Convert the words, "eight more than five times a number" into an expression. The term "eight more" means to add eight, and the term "five times a number" means multiply by five. Therefore, the expression $5x + 8$ is correct.

13. **B**

First, multiply the regular price by the percent off. 15% in decimal form is 0.15.

$30.00 × 0.15 = $4.50

Then, subtract the savings from the regular price.

$30.00 − $4.50 = $25.50

14. **D**

First, find the lowest common denominator for the numbers 8 and 7. The lowest common denominator is 56, because both 8 and 7 divide evenly into 56.

Then, put 56 into prime factored form. A prime number is a number that can only be divided by one and itself. A factor divides evenly into a number.

2 × 2 × 2 × 7 = 56

Therefore, 2 × 2 × 2 × 7 is the final answer.

15. **D**

This question is really asking you to find the square root of 400 and then the square root of 625. Remember, squaring a number and taking the square root of a number are opposite operations.

The square root of 400 is 20, because 20 × 20 = 400. The square root of 625 is 25, because 25 × 25 = 625. Therefore, the final answer is between 20 and 25.

16. **D**

The absolute value of a number is just the positive form of that number. The absolute value of −9 is simply 9.

17. **C**

First, find 10% of $24.00. $24.00 × 0.1 = $2.40

Then, add 1/2 of $2.40, which is $1.20, to $2.40.

$2.40 + $1.20 = $3.60

18. **C**

This question is really asking, "Which of the following answers can be divided evenly by the numbers 2, 6, and 7?" The answer is the number 42.

19. **D**

Round 311 to 300 and round 489 to 500. Then multiply:

300 × 500 = 150,000

20. **A**

In order to find the probability of a single outcome, you need to first list all possible outcomes from the experiment. If you flip a coin 3 times, there are 8 possible outcomes:

{HHH, HHT, HTH, THH, THT, HTT, TTH, TTT}

Each outcome has a 1/8 chance of occurring. The probability of getting 3 heads is 1/8.

21. **A**

In order to find Paul's mean score, add his scores for each of the four tests, and then divide by four.

3 + 6 + 9 + 10 = 28

28/4 = 7

22. **C**

Thursday has the smallest change in temperature over that of the previous day. The high temperature for Thursday is 60, while for Monday it is 65. The difference is only 5 degrees. On Tuesday (A), the temperature changes 15 degrees, on Wednesday (B), the temperature changes 10 degrees, and on Friday (D), the temperature changes 10 degrees.

23. **D**

If there is a 20% chance of rain, then there is a 80% chance that it *does not* rain. The probability that it *does not* rain is equal to 100% minus the probability that it does rain.

100% – 20% = 80%

24. **B**

Each flip of a coin is an independent event. Therefore, the probability that the coin lands heads is 1/2, no matter how many times it has just landed heads. The coin does not remember.

25. **C**

The mode is the most frequently occurring score. Because the number 5 occurs more often than any other number in the set, it is the mode score.

26. **D**

The number of complaints is not as important as the *average* number of complaints. This is because an average takes into consideration how long a company has been in business. BLUE TAXI company has 100/25, or an average of four complaints per month. However, GREEN TAXI company has 20/4, or an average of five complaints per month. Therefore, on the average, GREEN TAXI company has more complaints per month. It is misleading for a company to say that it has fewer complaints than another company when it has not been in business as long.

27. **B**

Since there are five cards, each card has a 0.2 probability of being selected.

This is because 1/5 = 0.2. Thus, the probability of selecting a heart is 0.2.

The probability of *not* selecting a heart is 1.0 – 0.2 = 0.80.

28. **B**

The coldest day of the week is Friday. Tuesday is the second coldest. Starting from the point on the graph that marks Tuesday, look left at the temperature axis that shows 50 degrees.

29. **A**

The amount of rainfall is determined by looking at the length of the bars. First, find the largest bar, which is December, and the second largest, which is November. The third largest is May. The fourth-largest amount of rainfall is October. Next, looking left from October to the rainfall axis, you can see that October had 7 inches of rain.

30. **B**

In order to find the median, you must first rank order the scores like this:

0, 2, 4, 5, 7, 8, 9.

The median value is the score in the middle. The median is 5.

31. **A**

Draw a line through the set of data points. Notice that low values of variable x go with high values of variable y, and that high values of variable x go with low values of variable y. Next, evaluate the truth of each possible answer.

The graph shows that as variable x increases, variable y decreases.

32. **C**

The amount of rainfall is determined by the length of the bars used to make the graph. First, find the shortest bar, which is February, and then the second shortest, which is January. The third-shortest bar is August. August has the third-lowest average monthly rainfall.

33. **A**

To divide a number by 3 means $x/3$. Add 5 to the result means plus 5. The answer is 9 means equals 9. The final answer is $x/3 + 5 = 9$.

34. **A**

The general equation for a line is $y = mx + b$, where m is the slope and b is the y-intercept. The slope is equal to rise over run, so the slope of the line in the graph is equal to $2/1$, or 2. The y-intercept is the point at which the line crosses the y-axis, so the y-intercept of the line is equal to 2. Therefore, the equation of the line is $y = 2x + 2$.

35. **C**

Draw a line through the set of data points. Notice that low temperatures go with low pollen count, and that high temperatures go with high pollen count. Next, evaluate the truth of each possible answer. The graph shows that as temperature goes up, pollen count tends to go up.

36. **B**

The graph of the function *y* equals *x* is the line shown.

(A) This is a graph of *y* equals negative *x* to the third power.

(C) This is a graph of *y* equals negative *x*.

(D) This is a graph of *y* equals *x* squared. This is a parabola.

37. **C**

$$(4xy^2)(8x^3y^4) = 32x^{1+3}y^{2+4} = 32x^4y^6$$

38. **D**

Solve for *x* means to get *x* by itself.

$$2x - 6 > 10$$

$$2x > 10 + 6$$

$$2x > 16$$

$$\frac{2x}{2} > \frac{16}{2}$$

$$x > 8$$

39. **B**

The variable on the bottom axis is "Balance in $1,000." The variable on the *y*-axis is "Interest rate in %." One line represents Bank A and one line represents Bank B. Notice that the two lines cross each other at $4,000. Bank A pays less interest than Bank B for balances of less than $4,000.

40. **D**

Let *g* equal the number of girls, and let *b* equal the number of boys. The number of boys as equal to three times the number of girls is expressed by $3 \times g = b$.

41. **B**

The variable on the *x*-axis is number of music CDs. The variable on the *y*-axis is total cost. The price of each CD can be read from finding one CD on the *x*-axis, going up until you hit the line, then reading the cost on the *y*-axis. The data point is half-way between $20 and $30. Therefore, one CD costs $25.

42. **B**

This question is asking you to substitute 6 for *x* and 7 for *y*. Then, perform the indicated operations in the equation to come up with a single number.

$$\frac{xy - 4}{2} - 5 = \frac{(6)(7) - 4}{2} - 5$$

$$= \frac{42 - 4}{2} - 5$$

$$= \frac{38}{2} - 5$$

$$= 19 - 5$$

$$= 14$$

43. **B**

$$(9xy^2z)(9xy^3z^4) = 81x^{1+1}y^{2+3}z^{1+4} = 81x^2y^5z^5$$

44. **D**

To solve for *x* means to get *x* by itself.

$$5x + 2 = 6$$
$$5x = 6 - 2$$
$$5x = 4$$
$$\frac{5x}{5} = \frac{4}{5}$$
$$x = \frac{4}{5}$$

45. **B**

Slope is equal to rise over run. In the figure, you can see that the rise is 4 and the run is 3. Therefore, the slope is 4 over 3 or 4/3.

46. **A**

Divide 16 by 3.2 in order to find out how many minutes it will take to fill the gas tank. 16 divided by 3.2 equals 5.

47. **C**

Draw a line through the points given but also extend this line upward. Next, find the year 2001 on the *x*-axis and then go up until you hit the line that you have drawn. Then, read the number of apples produced on the *y*-axis. The answer is 70,000.

48. **A**

To solve for *x* means to get *x* by itself.

$$\frac{x}{7} - 2 = 5$$

$$\frac{x}{7} = 5 + 2$$

$$\frac{x}{7} = 7$$

$$\frac{(7)x}{7} = 7(7)$$

$$x = 49$$

49. **D**

In order to calculate the average number of miles per gallon, you need to know two different variables. They are miles and gallons. This question gives you the number of miles traveled, but *not* the number of gallons used. The fact that the truck made 100 different deliveries is irrelevant information.

50. **C**

Average speed is expressed in terms of "miles per hour." *Per* means divide. Divide miles by hours:

120 divided by 2.5 equals 48

51. **C**

Multiply the number of centimeters in one inch by 100.

2.54 × 100 = 254

This is approximately equal to 250.

52. **C**

In order to answer this question, you need to use the Pythagorean theorem. The Pythagorean theorem tells you about the relationships between the length of the sides of a right triangle. The Pythagorean theorem is $a^2 + b^2 = c^2$, where a and b are the sides, and c is the hypotenuse. The hypotenuse is the side opposite the right angle. The present question is really asking you to find a.

$$a^2 + b^2 = c^2$$

$$a^2 + 12^2 = 13^2$$

$$a^2 + 144 = 169$$

$$a^2 = 169 - 144$$

$$a^2 = 25$$

$$\sqrt{a^2} = \sqrt{25}$$

$$a = 5$$

53. **B**

Divide the number of square feet by nine. 198 divided by 9 equals 22.

$$198/9 = 22$$

There are 22 square yards in 198 square feet.

54. **C**

See the shaded region as being made up of four separate triangles. Calculate the area of one triangle using the formula *one-half its base times its height*, or in formula form: 1/2*bh*. In the present problem, the base is 3 and the height is 3.

$$\frac{1}{2}(3)(3) = \frac{1}{2}(9) = 4.5$$

This is the area of one triangle. Since there are four triangles in the shaded region, multiply this area times four.

4.5 × 4 = 18

Next, calculate the area of the whole square that includes both the shaded and unshaded regions.

6 × 6 = 36

Lastly, in order to find the area of the unshaded region, subtract the smaller number from the larger number.

36 – 18 = 18

The final answer is 18 square inches.

55. **B**

This question is asking you to find the circumference of a circle. In this question you are given the length of the radius which is 8 inches. The diameter is equal to the radius times two, so the diameter is equal to 2(8) = 16 inches. Now, use the formula $C = \pi d$; $\pi = 3.14$

$C = 3.14(16) = 50.24 \approx 50$

The circumference of the circle is approximately equal to 50 inches.

56. **C**

Find the *x*-axis. Find the side of the figure closest to the *x*-axis and measure the distance that this side is from the *x*-axis. A reflection of the figure will put this side the same distance from the *x*-axis, but on the other side.

Also, notice the point labeled A. A reflection of this point across the *x*-axis will also be the same distance from the *x*-axis, but on the other side.

57. **A**

Use the formula 1/2*bh*.

$$\frac{1}{2}(12)(4) = \frac{1}{2}(48) = 24$$

The triangle has an area of 24 square inches. Note: The length of the side that equals 7 inches is irrelevant.

58. **C**

Multiply the number of cubic centimeters in one cubic inch by four.

$$4 \times 16.38 = 65.52$$

There are approximately 65.52 square centimeters in four cubic inches.

59. **D**

First, make use of the fact that the sum of the angles of any triangle is 180 degrees. The missing angle in the second triangle can be found by adding the two angles and then subtracting from 180.

$$80 + 30 = 110$$

$$180 - 110 = 70$$

60. **C**

The formula for the area of a triangle is 1/2*bh* where *b* equals base, and *h* equals height. The area of triangle A equals $\frac{1}{2}(10)(4) = \frac{1}{2}(40) = 20$. The area of triangle B equals $\frac{1}{2}(12)(5) = \frac{1}{2}(60) = 30$. Lastly, divide the area of triangle A by the area of triangle B, and put this fraction into lowest terms.

$$\frac{20}{30} = \frac{2}{3}$$

61. **B**

Plot the points given on an *x,y* graph. Then connect the nearest points. The figure created is a square.

62. **C**

In the scaled drawing, length is equal to 9 centimeters and width is equal to 4.5 centimeters. The scale is "1 centimeter is equal to 2 meters." So, the length is 18 meters and the width is 9 meters. Lastly, in order to find area, multiply length times width.

18 × 9 = 162

The final answer is 162 square meters.

63. **C**

See this figure as a square with a triangle removed. Calculate the area of the triangle. Area equals $\frac{1}{2}(6)(8) = \frac{1}{2}(48) = 24$. Then, calculate the area of the square. Area equals 10 × 10 = 100. Lastly, in order to find the area of the actual figure, subtract the area of the triangle from the area of the square.

100 – 24 = 76

64. **C**

First, calculate the area of the flower garden. Round 57 to 60, and round 52 to 50. Next, multiply: 60 × 50 = 3,000. The area of the flower garden is 3,000 square feet. Now, calculate the area of the lot. Round 104 to 100 and round 96 to 100 as well.

100 × 100 = 10,000

Lastly, in order to find the approximate area of the lawn, subtract the area of the flower garden from the area of the lot.

10,000 – 3,000 = 7,000

The lawn is approximately 7,000 square feet.

65. **C**

Use the formula: distance equals rate times time. In this question, you are given the rate, and you are given the distance. In order to solve for time, divide distance by rate thusly: 270 divided by 45 equals 6 hours. However, this question is asking for time in minutes. In order to convert hours into minutes, multiply by 60.

6 × 60 = 360

66. **D**

Calculate volume by multiplying height times width times length.

7 × 7 × 20 = 980

67. **D**

The formula given for the area of a circle is pi times *r* squared. Pi is approximately equal to 3.14 or more approximately 3, while *r* is equal to the radius of the circle. In this question, *r* is equal to 25.2 or approximately 25. The equation for area is pi times *r squared*. *r* squared equals *r* times *r*. Therefore, the approximate area of the circle is 3 × 25 × 25 = 1,875.

68. **A**

Determine the length of the trips in parts. For the first trip (A), there are 3 hours between 9:00 a.m. and 12:00 p.m., and there are 1 hour and 20 minutes between 12:00 p.m. and 1:20 p.m. So, the entire trip takes 4 hours and 20 minutes. Similarly, the second trip (B) takes 4 hours 35 minutes, the third trip (C) takes 4 hours and 25 minutes, and the last trip (D) takes 4 hours and 30 minutes. So, the first trip (A) is the shortest.

69. **A**

Solve for x means to get x by itself.

$$5(4x - 2) + 3(x + 1) = 39$$
$$20x - 10 + 3x + 3 = 39$$
$$23x - 7 = 39$$
$$23x = 39 + 7$$
$$23x = 46$$
$$\frac{23x}{23} = \frac{46}{23}$$
$$x = 2$$

70. **B**

In order to find the coordinates of the y-intercept of a line, let x equal 0 and solve for y.

$$8x - 10y = 40$$
$$8(0) - 10y = 40$$
$$-10y = 40$$
$$\frac{-10y}{-10} = \frac{40}{-10}$$
$$y = -4$$

Therefore, the coordinates of the y-intercept are (0, –4).

71. C

Two lines are parallel when they have the same slope.

72. D

This equation has an absolute value sign in it. An absolute value means the positive value of a number. The equation given is $|x + 8| = 12$. This is read, "the absolute value of $x + 8$ equals 12." There are two possible answers to this equation. Either,

$x + 8 = -12$ or $x + 8 = 12$

$x = -12 - 8$ or $x = 12 - 8$

$x = -20$ or $x = 4$

The final answer is $\{-20, 4\}$.

73. D

In order to find which point lies on the line expressed by an equation, plug each (x, y) point into the equation, one at a time, until you find a point that makes the equation true. The multiple choices are: $(1, 4)$ $(7, 3)$ $(3, 2)$ $(3, 7)$

$9x + 4y = 55$ is the equation given.

$9(1) + 4(4) = 25$ This does not equal 55.

$9(7) + 4(3) = 75$ This does not equal 55.

$9(3) + 4(2) = 35$ This does not equal 55.

$9(3) + 4(7) = 55$ *This does equal 55.* This point $(3, 7)$ falls on the line $9x + 4y = 55$

The final answer is the point $(3, 7)$.

74. B

In order to find the area of a rectangle, multiply width times length. The width is x, and the length is $x + 3$.

$$x(x + 3) = x^2 + 3x$$

75. **A**

Answering this question involves getting rid of the denominators by cross multiplying.

$$\frac{5}{x - 1} = \frac{8}{x}$$

$$\frac{5}{x - 1} \diagdown\!\!\!\!\diagup \frac{8}{x}$$

$$5x = 8(x - 1)$$

76. **D**

The equation $8|x| = 32$ has an absolute value sign in it. The absolute value of a number is always positive. There are two solutions to this equation. The two solutions are –4 and 4.

$8|X| = 32$

$8|-4| = 32$

$8|4| = 32$

The final answer is $\{-4, 4\}$

77. **B**

First, round the number 179 to 200. Second, round the number 222 also to 200. Then multiply thusly: 200 times 200 equals 40,000.

78. **D**

Solving this problem requires distributing the number in front of the parentheses across both terms inside of the parentheses.

$5(x + 3) = 5x + 15$

Therefore, $3x - 2 > 5(x + 3)$ is equivalent to $3x - 2 > 5x + 15$.

79. **C**

The general form for the equation of a line is $y = mx + b$ where m is the slope and b is the y-intercept. *Parallel lines have the same slope.* Inspect each of the multiple choices until you find a line that has the same slope.

In the equation $y = 3x - 5$, the slope is 3. Therefore, the line $y = 3x + 7$ is parallel to it.

80. **B**

This question is really asking, "Which of the following points will make both equations true?" In order to answer this question, try each (x, y) point, one at a time, until you find a point that makes *both* equations true.

The multiple choices are: (2, 7) (3, 12) (4, 17) (5, 22)

$y = 5x - 3$

$y = 4x$

$7 = 5(2) - 3$	$7 = 7$	true
$7 = 4(2)$	$7 = 8$	false
$12 = 5(3) - 3$	$12 = 12$	true
$12 = 4(3)$	$12 = 12$	true

The point (3, 12) makes both equations true.

17 = 5(4) – 3   17 = 17   true

17 = 4(4)   17 = 16   false

22 = 5(5) – 3   22 = 22   true

22 = 4(5)   22 = 20   false

The final answer is the point (3, 12).

Answer Sheet

Practice Test 1

1. Ⓐ Ⓑ Ⓒ Ⓓ
2. Ⓐ Ⓑ Ⓒ Ⓓ
3. Ⓐ Ⓑ Ⓒ Ⓓ
4. Ⓐ Ⓑ Ⓒ Ⓓ
5. Ⓐ Ⓑ Ⓒ Ⓓ
6. Ⓐ Ⓑ Ⓒ Ⓓ
7. Ⓐ Ⓑ Ⓒ Ⓓ
8. Ⓐ Ⓑ Ⓒ Ⓓ
9. Ⓐ Ⓑ Ⓒ Ⓓ
10. Ⓐ Ⓑ Ⓒ Ⓓ
11. Ⓐ Ⓑ Ⓒ Ⓓ
12. Ⓐ Ⓑ Ⓒ Ⓓ
13. Ⓐ Ⓑ Ⓒ Ⓓ
14. Ⓐ Ⓑ Ⓒ Ⓓ
15. Ⓐ Ⓑ Ⓒ Ⓓ
16. Ⓐ Ⓑ Ⓒ Ⓓ
17. Ⓐ Ⓑ Ⓒ Ⓓ
18. Ⓐ Ⓑ Ⓒ Ⓓ
19. Ⓐ Ⓑ Ⓒ Ⓓ
20. Ⓐ Ⓑ Ⓒ Ⓓ
21. Ⓐ Ⓑ Ⓒ Ⓓ
22. Ⓐ Ⓑ Ⓒ Ⓓ
23. Ⓐ Ⓑ Ⓒ Ⓓ
24. Ⓐ Ⓑ Ⓒ Ⓓ
25. Ⓐ Ⓑ Ⓒ Ⓓ
26. Ⓐ Ⓑ Ⓒ Ⓓ
27. Ⓐ Ⓑ Ⓒ Ⓓ

28. Ⓐ Ⓑ Ⓒ Ⓓ
29. Ⓐ Ⓑ Ⓒ Ⓓ
30. Ⓐ Ⓑ Ⓒ Ⓓ
31. Ⓐ Ⓑ Ⓒ Ⓓ
32. Ⓐ Ⓑ Ⓒ Ⓓ
33. Ⓐ Ⓑ Ⓒ Ⓓ
34. Ⓐ Ⓑ Ⓒ Ⓓ
35. Ⓐ Ⓑ Ⓒ Ⓓ
36. Ⓐ Ⓑ Ⓒ Ⓓ
37. Ⓐ Ⓑ Ⓒ Ⓓ
38. Ⓐ Ⓑ Ⓒ Ⓓ
39. Ⓐ Ⓑ Ⓒ Ⓓ
40. Ⓐ Ⓑ Ⓒ Ⓓ
41. Ⓐ Ⓑ Ⓒ Ⓓ
42. Ⓐ Ⓑ Ⓒ Ⓓ
43. Ⓐ Ⓑ Ⓒ Ⓓ
44. Ⓐ Ⓑ Ⓒ Ⓓ
45. Ⓐ Ⓑ Ⓒ Ⓓ
46. Ⓐ Ⓑ Ⓒ Ⓓ
47. Ⓐ Ⓑ Ⓒ Ⓓ
48. Ⓐ Ⓑ Ⓒ Ⓓ
49. Ⓐ Ⓑ Ⓒ Ⓓ
50. Ⓐ Ⓑ Ⓒ Ⓓ
51. Ⓐ Ⓑ Ⓒ Ⓓ
52. Ⓐ Ⓑ Ⓒ Ⓓ
53. Ⓐ Ⓑ Ⓒ Ⓓ
54. Ⓐ Ⓑ Ⓒ Ⓓ

55. Ⓐ Ⓑ Ⓒ Ⓓ
56. Ⓐ Ⓑ Ⓒ Ⓓ
57. Ⓐ Ⓑ Ⓒ Ⓓ
58. Ⓐ Ⓑ Ⓒ Ⓓ
59. Ⓐ Ⓑ Ⓒ Ⓓ
60. Ⓐ Ⓑ Ⓒ Ⓓ
61. Ⓐ Ⓑ Ⓒ Ⓓ
62. Ⓐ Ⓑ Ⓒ Ⓓ
63. Ⓐ Ⓑ Ⓒ Ⓓ
64. Ⓐ Ⓑ Ⓒ Ⓓ
65. Ⓐ Ⓑ Ⓒ Ⓓ
66. Ⓐ Ⓑ Ⓒ Ⓓ
67. Ⓐ Ⓑ Ⓒ Ⓓ
68. Ⓐ Ⓑ Ⓒ Ⓓ
69. Ⓐ Ⓑ Ⓒ Ⓓ
70. Ⓐ Ⓑ Ⓒ Ⓓ
71. Ⓐ Ⓑ Ⓒ Ⓓ
72. Ⓐ Ⓑ Ⓒ Ⓓ
73. Ⓐ Ⓑ Ⓒ Ⓓ
74. Ⓐ Ⓑ Ⓒ Ⓓ
75. Ⓐ Ⓑ Ⓒ Ⓓ
76. Ⓐ Ⓑ Ⓒ Ⓓ
77. Ⓐ Ⓑ Ⓒ Ⓓ
78. Ⓐ Ⓑ Ⓒ Ⓓ
79. Ⓐ Ⓑ Ⓒ Ⓓ
80. Ⓐ Ⓑ Ⓒ Ⓓ

Answer Sheet

Practice Test 2

1. Ⓐ Ⓑ Ⓒ Ⓓ	28. Ⓐ Ⓑ Ⓒ Ⓓ	55. Ⓐ Ⓑ Ⓒ Ⓓ	
2. Ⓐ Ⓑ Ⓒ Ⓓ	29. Ⓐ Ⓑ Ⓒ Ⓓ	56. Ⓐ Ⓑ Ⓒ Ⓓ	
3. Ⓐ Ⓑ Ⓒ Ⓓ	30. Ⓐ Ⓑ Ⓒ Ⓓ	57. Ⓐ Ⓑ Ⓒ Ⓓ	
4. Ⓐ Ⓑ Ⓒ Ⓓ	31. Ⓐ Ⓑ Ⓒ Ⓓ	58. Ⓐ Ⓑ Ⓒ Ⓓ	
5. Ⓐ Ⓑ Ⓒ Ⓓ	32. Ⓐ Ⓑ Ⓒ Ⓓ	59. Ⓐ Ⓑ Ⓒ Ⓓ	
6. Ⓐ Ⓑ Ⓒ Ⓓ	33. Ⓐ Ⓑ Ⓒ Ⓓ	60. Ⓐ Ⓑ Ⓒ Ⓓ	
7. Ⓐ Ⓑ Ⓒ Ⓓ	34. Ⓐ Ⓑ Ⓒ Ⓓ	61. Ⓐ Ⓑ Ⓒ Ⓓ	
8. Ⓐ Ⓑ Ⓒ Ⓓ	35. Ⓐ Ⓑ Ⓒ Ⓓ	62. Ⓐ Ⓑ Ⓒ Ⓓ	
9. Ⓐ Ⓑ Ⓒ Ⓓ	36. Ⓐ Ⓑ Ⓒ Ⓓ	63. Ⓐ Ⓑ Ⓒ Ⓓ	
10. Ⓐ Ⓑ Ⓒ Ⓓ	37. Ⓐ Ⓑ Ⓒ Ⓓ	64. Ⓐ Ⓑ Ⓒ Ⓓ	
11. Ⓐ Ⓑ Ⓒ Ⓓ	38. Ⓐ Ⓑ Ⓒ Ⓓ	65. Ⓐ Ⓑ Ⓒ Ⓓ	
12. Ⓐ Ⓑ Ⓒ Ⓓ	39. Ⓐ Ⓑ Ⓒ Ⓓ	66. Ⓐ Ⓑ Ⓒ Ⓓ	
13. Ⓐ Ⓑ Ⓒ Ⓓ	40. Ⓐ Ⓑ Ⓒ Ⓓ	67. Ⓐ Ⓑ Ⓒ Ⓓ	
14. Ⓐ Ⓑ Ⓒ Ⓓ	41. Ⓐ Ⓑ Ⓒ Ⓓ	68. Ⓐ Ⓑ Ⓒ Ⓓ	
15. Ⓐ Ⓑ Ⓒ Ⓓ	42. Ⓐ Ⓑ Ⓒ Ⓓ	69. Ⓐ Ⓑ Ⓒ Ⓓ	
16. Ⓐ Ⓑ Ⓒ Ⓓ	43. Ⓐ Ⓑ Ⓒ Ⓓ	70. Ⓐ Ⓑ Ⓒ Ⓓ	
17. Ⓐ Ⓑ Ⓒ Ⓓ	44. Ⓐ Ⓑ Ⓒ Ⓓ	71. Ⓐ Ⓑ Ⓒ Ⓓ	
18. Ⓐ Ⓑ Ⓒ Ⓓ	45. Ⓐ Ⓑ Ⓒ Ⓓ	72. Ⓐ Ⓑ Ⓒ Ⓓ	
19. Ⓐ Ⓑ Ⓒ Ⓓ	46. Ⓐ Ⓑ Ⓒ Ⓓ	73. Ⓐ Ⓑ Ⓒ Ⓓ	
20. Ⓐ Ⓑ Ⓒ Ⓓ	47. Ⓐ Ⓑ Ⓒ Ⓓ	74. Ⓐ Ⓑ Ⓒ Ⓓ	
21. Ⓐ Ⓑ Ⓒ Ⓓ	48. Ⓐ Ⓑ Ⓒ Ⓓ	75. Ⓐ Ⓑ Ⓒ Ⓓ	
22. Ⓐ Ⓑ Ⓒ Ⓓ	49. Ⓐ Ⓑ Ⓒ Ⓓ	76. Ⓐ Ⓑ Ⓒ Ⓓ	
23. Ⓐ Ⓑ Ⓒ Ⓓ	50. Ⓐ Ⓑ Ⓒ Ⓓ	77. Ⓐ Ⓑ Ⓒ Ⓓ	
24. Ⓐ Ⓑ Ⓒ Ⓓ	51. Ⓐ Ⓑ Ⓒ Ⓓ	78. Ⓐ Ⓑ Ⓒ Ⓓ	
25. Ⓐ Ⓑ Ⓒ Ⓓ	52. Ⓐ Ⓑ Ⓒ Ⓓ	79. Ⓐ Ⓑ Ⓒ Ⓓ	
26. Ⓐ Ⓑ Ⓒ Ⓓ	53. Ⓐ Ⓑ Ⓒ Ⓓ	80. Ⓐ Ⓑ Ⓒ Ⓓ	
27. Ⓐ Ⓑ Ⓒ Ⓓ	54. Ⓐ Ⓑ Ⓒ Ⓓ		

Index